Peace to you,

Jeff Archer

Elena 6/16

FINDING HOME WITH THE BEATLES, BOB DYLAN, AND BILLY GRAHAM

A Memoir of Growing Up Inside the Billy Graham Evangelistic Association

JESS ARCHER

WESTBOW
PRESS®
A DIVISION OF THOMAS NELSON
& ZONDERVAN

Scripture taken from the Holy Bible, NEW INTERNATIONAL VERSION®.
Copyright © 1973, 1978, 1984 by Biblica, Inc. All rights reserved worldwide.
Used by permission. NEW INTERNATIONAL VERSION® and NIV® are
registered trademarks of Biblica, Inc. Use of either trademark for the offering
of goods or services requires the prior written consent of Biblica US, Inc.

Author photo by Janice Reyes Photography

WestBow Press books may be ordered through booksellers or by contacting:

WestBow Press
A Division of Thomas Nelson & Zondervan
1663 Liberty Drive
Bloomington, IN 47403
www.westbowpress.com
1 (866) 928-1240

Because of the dynamic nature of the Internet, any web addresses or
links contained in this book may have changed since publication and
may no longer be valid. The views expressed in this work are solely those
of the author and do not necessarily reflect the views of the publisher,
and the publisher hereby disclaims any responsibility for them.

Any people depicted in stock imagery provided by Thinkstock are models,
and such images are being used for illustrative purposes only.
Certain stock imagery © Thinkstock.

ISBN: 978-1-5127-2161-4 (sc)
ISBN: 978-1-5127-2162-1 (hc)
ISBN: 978-1-5127-2160-7 (e)

Library of Congress Control Number: 2015919466

Print information available on the last page.

WestBow Press rev. date: 12/16/2015

For my earthly father
and
for the late Thom Williams

TABLE OF CONTENTS

Blackbird singing in the dead of night,
Take these broken wings and learn to fly.
All your life,
You were only waiting for this moment
to arise.

—The Beatles

IN EVERY NEIGHBORHOOD

In every neighborhood there is a tennis shoe looped around a telephone wire, a tilting mailbox, and a bicycle left out in the rain.

And in every neighborhood is a house for rent.

My father moved his family of six around the world for fifteen years because he felt that God had called him to work for Reverend Billy Graham.

I believed in that calling, even as I suffered for it as a child. As my body grew up, my eyes saw what can only be described as a movement of God's Spirit under the stadium lights during countless Billy Graham crusades. But of my father's four children, I struggled the most to reconcile myself with the life we lived. I was a broken blackbird in the night who sang a tearful song and who would not rise from the challenges of our kind of life until the dawn of my young adulthood.

In a bedroom of one of those houses for rent is a brown cardboard packing box with my name on it, printed in all caps in my father's definitive, assertive hand. The box sits on beige carpet in a freshly cleaned bedroom, where it waits for me—in the dark of night, in the light of day, in the quietude of "no one lives here *yet*." The objects inside the box hold their breath until I arrive. When I come, I will step into that house like a blind girl feeling her way. For the first time, my hand will brush the walls through every room.

I will find my new bedroom and the box waiting for me. I will pull up the tape and start over again.

CHAPTER 1

ALL YOU NEED IS LOVE

As a child, I felt that my father's dramatic conversion to Christianity was just like one from the Bible…only his happened in the seventies and there were bell-bottoms—and lots of drugs. Otherwise he could have been Lazarus rising from the dead. "Jesus called out in a loud voice, 'Lazarus, come out!'"

When my father told his story, I remembered again that the gospel calls us out, calls us straight out of death and into new life.

It was my father's story of his conversion to Christianity that reignited my own faith over and over again in evangelism, and in the oddity of our nomadic life as we traveled the world with Billy Graham.

When Dad told his story, I wanted people to hear it. I wanted people to get the point. And the point, after all, was Jesus. Dad's story was about people praying for him behind his back, people loving him with a gentle shove toward the cross. And in some ways it was about the best music in the world, composed by the Beatles and, later, Bob Dylan. Because of my father's conversion story, I felt he could be trusted for hitching our wagon to Billy Graham's.

My father, Richard James Marshall, could have been the Warren, Michigan, blond, blue-eyed poster boy of the 1950s. Of German descent, and son of the local school board president, Dad was smart—and the dashing eldest of three Marshall kids.

The only solidly Christian thing in my father's childhood was his maternal grandparents. His grandfather started each day at sunup by reading the Bible. Dad's grandmother used to slip into his room when he was a very small child to hold him and sing "Jesus Loves Me" in a whisper. But that simple, subtle thread hung loose and disconnected. It was of no value to him until college.

Dad's childhood was a mostly tense one. His father was prone to outbursts of verbal abuse and was virtually unavailable when it came to offering praise or encouragement. His parents fought openly and often. Long car rides to visit Dad's grandparents in Florida were spent in a smoke-filled Chevy with the windows up, his father puffing silently and his mother dissatisfied and feeling rejected.

My mother, Becki Lynn Decker, on the other hand, was raised with probably more overt Christianity than anyone should claim—a bit of an overdose of all things "born again." Her father, my papa Decker, was a midwestern Baptist preacher in the one-traffic-light town of Gladwin, Michigan. Before that, he was a preacher for an even longer time in Deckerville, Michigan.

Every Sunday morning and evening, their family of seven attended church, where my grammy Decker faithfully played the church organ. Mom's maternal grandparents had been missionaries on the Alaskan Aleutian Islands and in Mexico, and her uncle directed with gusto the Good News Camp for Kids, where Mom had first asked Jesus into her heart at age six. She wore sequined eyeglasses as a teenager and was voted homecoming queen in her senior year.

By the time my mother was ready for college, her faith in Christ and every jumper she wore had been lovingly hand-stitched. She was a Baptist-born American sweetheart.

My father raced to college in 1970 in a state of panic and for one reason only: to avoid the Vietnam draft. The summer after he graduated from high school, the US government Selective Service's national lottery was held. Men whose birthdays fell within the first hundred dates drawn would be eligible for military service in Vietnam.

Dad's birthday was number 6. His only hope to avoid enlistment was to enroll in a university.

He had applied to four schools in Michigan, and he attended the first one that accepted him, which happened to be Central Michigan University. On his first day of college, as my grandparents pulled away from his dorm and waved good-bye in their Chevy Capri station wagon, eighteen-year-old Rick Marshall cried. He was there to avoid a cause, but he had no inkling how to find one.

Within hours of his first day of dorm life, his suite mate burst into his room. "Who wants to get high?"

Dad leapt at the offer. For the next three years, he let drugs take him down a dismal, bleak hole.

My parents met in 1971, in the fall of their sophomore year of college at CMU, and although my father was attracted to my mother physically, he was emotionally detached from her. There was no center to his life from which to draw out love. When Dad had entered college as a freshman, his parents were already on the verge of divorce. Subconsciously he sensed their layered distance from each other, and it deeply depressed him. During one winter break, he took Mom home to meet them.

When she asked, "Why does your mother sleep on the sofa in the basement?" Dad could only answer lamely,

"I guess she's sick."

"How long has she been 'sick'?"

"Five years, I think."

It was all just more reason to escape into drugs.

Dad had already leapt into the anti–Vietnam War scene on campus, first blindly participating in rallies, and then vehemently leading them. Pot sometimes helped him escape his mounting depression, and LSD thrust him so far from his own cynical conscious mind that he took the risks. He began taking art classes, specifically oil painting, hoping to unearth a hidden talent or at least tap into his mounting anger and disillusionment in a world at war.

His paintings were dark and cold, showing stark figures whose expressions reflected internal agony. His professors commended him and encouraged his talents. He stayed in the studio late into the night with friends. He wore his hair long and was voted student body president in 1973, yet he had no idea what he wanted out of life.

Then, one very cold December night in 1973, Dad attended a film festival on campus and took some LSD. Halfway through one of the films, he started to fall apart from a psychedelic trip. The film suddenly appeared in 3-D, and it seemed as though his legs didn't work anymore. Everything in his vision was blurred and swirled.

He stumbled out of the auditorium. For the rest of his life, he would wonder just what took place in the next series of minutes. Did he fall down? Did he step into traffic and get hit by a car? All he knew is that someone began calling his name.

"Rick, what's happened? Your leg!" It was Diane Morris, a young woman with whom he painted in the art studio. He had collapsed on the pavement by the side of the road. His brain registered searing pain running up his entire leg and lower back.

"Rick, what just happened to you?" Diane tried to help him up.

He had no answers. Under that clear, cold night sky, he dragged himself a hundred yards to Merrill Hall and up three flights of stairs to his dorm room.

Dad didn't know it at the time, but his roommate and best childhood friend, Steve Salowitz, had just become a Christian. Steve had been praying for several months that God would get my father's attention, would cause Rick to come face-to-face with his brokenness.

In his collapsed position, Dad managed one faint knock on the door. Steve heard and answered. As Steve opened the door, Dad looked into his dorm room—and that's when he saw it: intense, pulsating colors and thousands upon thousands of musical notes rushing toward him. It was the Beatles' "All You Need Is Love" on the hi-fi. His eyes saw the black velvet notes pour from the speakers in tidal waves, soaring toward him like blackbirds, grazing and caressing his head. Out flew the music, a lullaby, an anthem—the exact musical notation of his heart's cry: *Nowhere you can be that isn't where you're meant to be ... it's easy.*

Then John Lennon, like a red-robed prophet in my father's vision, softly marched out with the last refrain: "Nothing you can sing that can't be sung. Nothing you can do, but you can learn how to be you in time. It's easy."

The song closed with the Fab Four clapping like gospel saints and with "What Child Is This?" (Greensleeves) humming on strings as Steve got ready to rush my father to the hospital.

Because of insurance reasons, Dad was forced to call his parents at the hospital. The doctor who examined him asked him point-blank, "Have you been doing drugs, young man?"

"No!" Dad lied, terrified that his parents would find out. As he lay shivering in pain on the X-ray table, the strangest memory came to him, of his grandmother singing "Jesus Loves Me." He hadn't even known he remembered it. How badly he needed her song now.

The injury Dad experienced that decisive night was never fully explained by doctors. To be sure, he wasn't able to walk for weeks afterward. Physical therapy was prescribed, and because he couldn't walk, he endured the humility of riding his childhood banana seat bike to class every day for a month afterward.

Dad turned back to Mom for solace and a second chance at a relationship. He began to pursue her more openly. In response, she took him home to meet her big, boisterous Christian family. He'd never met people like them before: genuine and strangely joyful. He wanted that.

On New Year's Eve 1973, my mother asked Dad to attend a "watch service" at her father's church in Gladwin. "It will be fun—lots of games and food."

"All right," Dad agreed. He figured they would stay an hour or two and then slip out to find a real New Year's Eve party.

Mom was right: the party was fun. And just as Dad began to forget he was in a church, my grandfather switched gears and ushered everyone into pew seats. He began to speak about life changes and about how no person has the power to change his or her life without Christ. It was minutes before midnight.

Dad's neck began to sweat. He felt angry, betrayed. *Who has told him all about me?* he thought to himself. He wanted to flee the room in the worst way, but he was stuck. On his left was his girlfriend, and on his right was her grandmother. For the next minute he worked to slither down into his seat, hoping to hide behind the bun hairdos of the old maids in front of him.

But he could avoid himself no longer.

"Some of you here will be the same person one year from now that you are tonight, unless Christ changes you from within." My grandfather's voice pierced the room and my young father's heart. Something in the latter gave up the fight. He couldn't change the world; he couldn't change his university; he couldn't even change himself. His life was a stagnant, lonely darkness. He was just like the figures in his own paintings. Without another thought, he stood up. "My life is a mess. I need Jesus Christ."

Something mysterious and wonderful happened to my father that night. My grandfather gently ushered Dad to a side room in the sanctuary, where they prayed on their knees together. It was the early hours of New Year's Day, 1974 and the beginning of my father's new life.

As a new Christian, Dad was drastically changed. He found himself voracious for spiritual food. He began by reading Francis Schaeffer's *Basic Bible Studies* book. Christianity became a crashing, cleansing wave.

In the next few months he spent hours simply reading the Bible, something he'd never imagined doing before that night at my grandfather's church. Dad's outward life began to reflect an inward peace. His abrasive language changed. He no longer abused drugs. He spoke passionately to those who'd listen about the grace of God.

He experienced transformation from the inside out. The only thing he took with him into his new life as a Christian was his favorite music: the Beatles and Bob Dylan.

A man by the name of Mark Bonham had been at the New Year's Eve service the night my father declared his desperate need for Christ. Mark had contacts at CMU. One day shortly after the New Year's Eve service, Dad got a call. "Hi, Rick. You don't know me, but I know you."

Mark put Dad in touch with Chuck Romine, a serious and determined Christian man who worked for the Navigators at CMU, a Christian discipleship group founded after World War II by Dawson Trotman. For the next three years, Chuck Romine dedicated himself to my father's spiritual growth. Week after week he walked my young father through the Scriptures, challenging him to read the Bible every single day. Chuck watched Dad bloom measurably in his understanding of Scripture and in his ability to communicate it to others with freshness and sincerity. One night Chuck told Dad, "You know, I can see you working with Billy Graham."

"What?" Dad replied in disbelief. "You mean the preacher on TV?"

My parents were married in May 1974 while they were still students at CMU. Dad, with blond hair down to his shoulders, and Mom, a slim, dark Victorian cameo in a cream-colored high-collared dress. They exuded 1970s romance and student poverty.

The ceremony was held in Gladwin, at Papa Decker's Round Lake Baptist Church. The reception venue was Gladwin Middle School's cafeteria. The boisterous German ladies of the church prepared mini hot dogs and Waldorf salad, and Mom's aunt Cindy made a tilting, three-tier carrot cake. The big honeymoon was a trip to Dad's grandmother's tiny bungalow in Florida, where he fished and Mom posed for country-girl photos in the rickety two-seater boat. They were both twenty-one and practically penniless, with one year of college still left to complete.

The year before I was born, Mom's uncle Joe Lathrop, at one of Mom's family reunions in the summer of 1976, approached Dad with an idea. Uncle Joe had worked for Luis Palau, an Argentine evangelist of some renown. Uncle Joe thought that his niece's fiery hippie husband had vision and leadership skills and needed a larger scope for his talents. Uncle Joe pitched Dad the idea of working for evangelist Billy Graham.

"That guy on TV?" Dad was miffed again, recalling that Chuck Romine had suggested the same thing. He couldn't conceive of the idea, but Joe seemed to be so much in earnest that Dad said he'd consider it.

Uncle Joe made some phone calls and scheduled for Dad to meet with Sterling Huston, Billy Graham's director of North American crusades. The two met for lunch at the Hilton Hotel in Troy, Michigan, to discuss Christian ministry. Sterling Huston was the epitome of his dashing name: a tall, articulate man with (ironically) a sterling silver white man's afro. Dad was terribly nervous. He'd never ordered food from a hotel restaurant.

Dr. Huston, cordial but intimidating, was intelligent and organized. And during their lunch conversation, Dad fumbled with words about ministry and evangelism like he'd never even heard the terms. He was pretty sure he'd never hear from Huston again.

Three years later, in April 1980, Dr. Huston called my dad from a pay phone in JFK airport. "Rick, we haven't forgotten about you. Are you still interested in Billy Graham's crusade ministry? We've been keeping your name before the Lord in prayer."

He invited Dad and Mom to spend two days in Indianapolis, Indiana, at the May 1980 crusade to meet the people behind the scenes who made a Billy Graham crusade work.

"Watch and listen. See if this is a calling you can find yourself in."

Of course, my young, exuberant parents were impressed. Those two days were like nothing they had ever seen before—fast-paced, professional, life-altering. Thousands of people in the stadium hung on to Mr. Graham's every word. My parents got to sit on the platform with the special guests on the second night, just ten feet away from Mr. Graham. Of course Dad would say yes to Dr. Huston's question.

Sterling Huston called Dad two weeks after the Indianapolis crusade to hire him, but with a disclaimer: "This will be a mentorship position. You'll be more like an intern, learning about making preparations for a Billy Graham crusade. Billy is really slowing down. He has one, maybe two years left of this kind of large-scale evangelism."

Billy Graham was sixty-one years old when my father began working for him, which was in August 1980. At that time Billy Graham had already been preaching for over thirty-five years, since after World War II. He called his public meetings "crusades" as a reverent nod to the passion of the early Crusaders' quest for Jerusalem, though this name would change after September 11, 2001, to "missions."

Graham's evangelical crusades had started as tent-style revivals in the 1940s, when he preached the message of salvation from sin in Christ and invited listeners to make a personal response to Christ's invitation in the gospels, namely, "For God so loved the world that he gave his one and only Son, that whoever believes in him shall have eternal life" (John 3:16).

At Billy Graham crusades, this personal response took the form of an altar call, where people were asked to come forward publicly to the front of the arena. Graham recognized the neutralizing safety of a large crowd, its anonymity. Stepping out in faith toward an invisible God required courage. Billy Graham called on that courage within his millions of listeners. "I want you to do something very humbling tonight as a step of faith. I want you to get up out of your seats and come forward publicly, and to say by your coming, 'I need Christ in my life.'"

Then he would lead these inquirers, standing in the thousands on the stadium floor, through a simple prayer of repentance from sins, inviting Jesus to come into their lives. These tender hearts were then given a copy of the gospel of John or a Bible study booklet by trained volunteer counselors who could pray further with them and help lead them toward a church in their community that could disciple them in the Christian faith.

It was for this multifaceted work that my father was hired by the Billy Graham Evangelistic Association (BGEA) in 1980, when I was just three years old.

What started for my father as an internship position with the Billy Graham Evangelistic Association ended twenty-five years later with him as the director of crusades for his boss, his confidant, and his by then close friend, Reverend Billy Graham.

As a little girl, I heard my father tell his story over and over again at Billy Graham crusade rallies and at churches peppered around cities where we lived. His point was to help people understand that just because he worked for Billy Graham, this fact didn't make him a saint—and that it didn't take a saint to invite someone to a Billy Graham crusade.

One time, when I was about ten, Dad asked me after a speaking engagement, "Well, how'd I do, Jess?"

I told him the truth: "I really like the part about you in college, when you saw the Beatles music fly out of the speakers."

He laughed. "Well, that was mostly the drugs, Jess."

I didn't think that mattered. And secretly, I knew my father didn't think it mattered either. Dad always made sure to tell that part of the story because he knew, and so I learned from him, that Christ is right there in the farthest, deepest dead end of the rabbit hole, staring right back at you with warm, liquid eyes, ready to say, "Okay, kid, let's turn around and go back out together."

Christ behind us. Christ before us. Christ anointing our heads with wave upon wave of musical notes that compose the message, "All you need is love!" Dad emerged out of his rabbit hole of drugs, anger, and confusion and came into the light of Christ's indwelling.

The music he saw pour from those speakers was the Beatles. Since the time I can remember, the Fab Four sounded like church music to me. In all of God's mysterious ways, the Beatles were the choir singing my family along our journey of life on the road with Billy Graham.

My father's true story of conversion to Christianity and the origins of his twenty-five years of work with Billy Graham helped me and my father both to grasp the seen and the unseen. I learned to believe that Billy Graham was called by God. My earthly father caught the echo of that calling and followed. Billy Graham, Dad and Mom were in the grip of God, and so, by default, was I. I wasn't lost. I wasn't home either, but I wasn't lost.

CHAPTER 2

MY FATHER'S CRUSADE

"Oh, your dad is like John the Baptist, preparing the way for the one who is to come!" People liked to say this to me, pleased with themselves for having thought of the analogy. I appreciated the sentiment, but Billy Graham was not Jesus, and my father did not live off milk and honey or wear animal skins. Dad believed that Billy Graham was called to preach but that he was a fallible man like any other. So was my father, for that matter.

Dad worked hard to hone his talents as a visionary, organizer, and leader, but he also chose a career and ministry path with the BGEA, one that by its very unstable nature created fallout for his family. If it weren't for my father's willingness to listen to his children, then the degree of anxiety I experienced as a child from our transient lifestyle might have been irreparable.

After our first move with the Billy Graham Evangelistic Association, to Calgary, Alberta, Billy Graham himself asked my father, "Rick, will you continue this work? Will you and Becki move your family with us again?"

Dad and Mom got on their knees and prayed for layered protection over their family. They bought a map of the world to hang on the kitchen wall, and they said yes to Billy Graham again. I was four years old in the spring of our year in Calgary.

One night at dinner I spoke up, saying, "I want a best friend when we move to Spokane."

Mom and Dad arched their brows, impressed by the utterance, and said, "Well, why don't we pray for that?" I did, and they prayed as backup support.

A few months later, Dad was in Spokane, Washington, searching the suburbs for a rental house for his family of six. Time was ticking. He had to make a choice, but none of the options seemed just right. On the last day of his search, he sat outside one last house, waiting for the realtor to arrive. He had the windows down in his rental car. He had closed his eyes for just a moment when a small voice called out to him, "Mister, are you gonna buy this house?" It was a little girl outside his car door.

"No, but I think I might rent it and live here for a while."

"My name is Jenny. I'm four. Do you have any kids that are four?"

Sometimes listening to God simply means agreeing with your child's prayers before God. Jenny and I became the very best of friends that year in Spokane. We lived next door to each other for one year. She was my first friend.

There is an affection for the first of anything good in life: your first love, your first car, your firstborn. Jenny was my first friend in a childhood procession of friends to come, friends who lined up on sidewalks of the world and waved good-bye as my family drove out of sight.

In those early years with the BGEA, Dad flew around the United States often, learning from others in the organization how to think of the Great Commission in pragmatic ways. He began to learn how to take stock of the evangelistic needs of a city; how to bolster the local church leaders in their efforts to meet those needs; how to fit thousands of people onto a stadium floor, people who might want to come forward in response to Mr. Graham's invitation; how not to violate city fire codes but simultaneously let the Spirit move...a tricky sort of balance, a balance that necessitated sensitivity.

My father had a posture for listening to God. It looked like an open Bible, a pen in hand, and his eyes cast off into middle distance, that area not so far away as to suggest idealism but not so close as to miss the bigger picture.

By the time we lived in Paris, France, in 1985, we had moved five times with the BGEA. Dad and his team had organized every detail of the crusades in five major cities across North America, but in Paris my father was made acutely aware of his cultural deficits.

At business dinners he could not order from the French menus himself, nor did he have any idea how to eat escargot. The wines, the cheeses, they seemed to overflow into les boulevards, of which he could hardly name one. He trudged home from the subways at night to our apartment in Neuilly, where he and Mom laughed about their foibles from the day. They slept the vulnerable, exhausted sleep of foreigners.

But even amid all that got lost in translation, Dad was listening. Early on in his preparation for the Mission France crusade, he sensed a mounting disunity among the reformed denominations. There was a brittle quality to their conversations about which venue should host the mission. The two cochairs, Charles Guillot and André Thobois, were at the center of the disputes, refusing to compromise with each other. Dad prayed and then prayed some more. After a time, he felt confirmed in his heart that he needed to make a direct appeal to Mr. Graham for intervention, or else there would not be a Mission France.

In September 1985, it just so happened that Mr. Graham was going to be in Paris for two days, en route back to the United States, having just completed a mission in Eastern Europe. It was Dad's chance to speak with him about the matters on his heart and mind.

It was a postcardlike fall day in Paris. Dad sat on a carpet of lush grass, the Eiffel Tower just behind him. Billy Graham and Blair Carlson, the latter being regional director of Mission France, sat on a bench in front of him. Looking up, Dad told Mr. Graham all that he understood about the disputes between the Mission France leaders.

"What should I do?" was Mr. Graham's humble question.

Dad took a deep breath, stared off into that middle distance, and then said, "I think you need to write a letter."

The following is from Billy Graham's letter to André Thobois:

September 27, 1985

Since being here, in a very strange and remarkable way, God has confirmed to my heart that we will hold the meetings in Bercy in 1986. Also, many prayers are being answered. I had put out some "fleeces," and it seems that all of them have been answered except the one regarding total unity on the committee. Thus I believe it is God's time for France, it is God's moment to return. I did not feel this way before I arrived. I know that there are obstacles to overcome, but in the work of Evangelism we are invading Satan's territory. In evangelism we cease being defensive, we go on the offense. Thus Satan is going to put every obstacle in our way. He never gives up without a fight. My beloved friend, I have had to face this situation in every campaign I have ever held anywhere in the world. I challenge you, Brother Thobois, to stay in and help work out the differences between the brethren.

André Thobois did just as Mr. Graham asked of him. As a result, the Mission France week in September 1986 was a thing of beauty. Thousands of Parisians streamed through the doors of the Palais Omnisport de Bercy. Mr. Graham preached the gospel of Christ with fervor and humility—his paradoxical trademark. Over a hundred thousand people attended, and over seven thousand men and women answered the small knock of God at their hearts. As many people responded to the gospel in eight days as attended all the Protestant churches in Paris at the time.

There was another posture to my father's listening, and this one had to do with his favorite music. On our long road trips from city to city, the only music my father ever allowed us to listen to was either that of the Beatles or Bob Dylan. He said his ears couldn't handle anything else.

He tapped out the rhythm of "You Gotta Serve Somebody" on the steering wheel as I watched him from the backseat. I knew whom this life of ours served, and it wasn't Billy Graham. My father's listening posture seemed to say, *I remember again whom I serve, and I trust you, Father.* If Dad trusted God's direction, then I could trust Dad.

So, one night I confessed with hot, burning tears that I had become afraid of many things. It was hard to let them out. *Will naming them make them worse?* But Dad was ready.

He took a deep breath and turned to face me so that I could see my blue eyes reflected in his. He said, "I am afraid of many things too, Jess, especially riding in airplanes." I wiped my eyes. This was new information. Something very specific frightened my father, made him feel that hollow pit in his stomach that I felt all the time.

I had assumed he walked around all day long in a kind of verve, his crusade to spread the gospel shaping a hedge of peace around him wherever he went. But it was not apparently so. He experienced exposed moments of fear, just like I did. It was alarming to me, and I said nothing at the time. But as days passed, I formed a plan. I would surprise Dad with a note in his briefcase every time he traveled on an airplane. The more I thought about it, the more pleased with the idea I became. It would be my mission to soothe my sensitive father.

I didn't know at the time how desperately, in the years to come, I would be the one who required soothing from paralyzing anxiety.

CHAPTER 3

MY MOTHER'S CRUSADE

The bones of a house are not what's admired. And it wasn't my mother's work that was admired by people we met when we moved to a new city with the Billy Graham Evangelistic Association. For a long time, I didn't admire her either. I fought against my mother.

Only as an adult did I realize that all those years I pushed, she never crumbled. She was what held our loose, disjointed life together. The bones of a house give; they ease imperceptibly to the eye; they adjust to the elements. My mother was a master at adjusting.

My father's job was to prepare the way for Billy Graham to speak the gospel message to people of many cities. Dad was busy every day leading a team of people in big, sweeping campaigns toward this goal. Dad's to-do list itself induced awe: (1) Train thousands of volunteers; (2) Tour local stadiums; (3) Arrange print media advertising.

It was big work in terms of numbers and significance. It was like weather that everyone in a city feels and talks about. Billboards announcing Billy Graham's imminent arrival were my father's doing. Radio ads and TV ads pointed back at my dad and his job.

But when it came to my mother, you had to step across the threshold of our house to see her genius at work. You had to get to know us or bother to ask yourself, *How in the world does a family of six manage to move cities every nine months?* The answer was my mother; she was the strength supporting my father's mission. And she did it all with less than 60 percent eyesight.

Mom was born with a degenerative eye disease. One time she told me that as a child, she thought it was normal to have legs and knees covered in scratches and bruises from falling. She figured everyone tripped over stuff they didn't see. When she was nine years old, her parents took her to an eye doctor who stood back to marvel after the examination, "Young lady, you are blind!"

"How blind?" I used to ask, worried.

"Well," she'd say in her typically chipper voice while pointing at her left eye, "in this one it's like looking through wax paper." That wasn't comforting.

"And the other one?" I'd hesitantly ask, afraid to know the truth.

"The other eye is tricky. It's probably for you like looking through a toilet paper tube. No peripheral vision."

It was an impossible setup. She was besieged from the start. It was a handicap that should have been her easy out. No adventures for her. She should keep her routine simple, consistent, and free of clutter, or else. Or else what? She might get hurt?

Not my mother. From the time she was five years old, she wanted to be a missionary, the kind with an iron heart and a baffling surrender to God—like Jim and Elisabeth Elliot, like Amy Carmichael. As a teenager she read their biographies, and her heart yearned to serve God in foreign countries as they did. She had no intention of letting her eye disease stop her.

She developed throughout her teenage and young adult years incredible coping skills for her handicap. She stayed positive.

I cannot recall my mother ever once being in a plain old bad mood. "If I wanted to sulk about my eyes, what good would that do? I'd just be miserable *and* blind." Her pleasant disposition had a way of calming my fears about her limited eyesight. Before I knew it, I was caught up in whatever funny story she was telling or in whatever brilliant game she was inventing for us kids to play.

People liked my mom right away. She was unpretentious. It was the midwestern girl in her. She was pretty and just naïve enough to ask endearing questions. And in our travels, when my father slipped into brooding melancholy, she stayed up on the horse and called out the shots.

Mother dealt with whatever came her way by staying in the Word. She kept our family Bible on the kitchen table. I'd often find her there trying to read the small print, squinting at it, pulling the book back far, bringing it in close, like some kind of diamond merchant—examining and tilting it in her limited eye sight, to better absorb the beauty and richness of scripture.

And she stayed busy. Mom raised four children while hopscotching through ten cities around the globe.

My mother's eyesight was blurry, but her vision for ministry with the BGEA was crystal clear. She wanted to serve God by helping evangelize the people we met in each city. She wanted to support my dad by providing him with the comforts of home, and she wanted to transition her four children from city to city as smoothly as possible. During our fifth move with the BGEA, to Anchorage, Alaska, I saw some of those desires come to light.

One day, a voice came over the loudspeaker in my cozy classroom at Northern Lights Elementary School, a woman's voice that barely masked anxiety. It was our school principal, and she was insistent. "Everyone, get underneath your desks. We are experiencing an earthquake." I obeyed.

The concrete floor was cold and wet from the slush on our boots. To me, *earthquake* conjured up only a photograph of broken houses in a library book. I reached out and placed my hand, palm down, on the floor. And then my arm moved in a thrust, this way and then that way. My body shook too, although I sat crouching as still as I could. It seemed I held my breath for as long as the earthquake lasted. There was a final rumble under the ground, like massive construction beneath our knees, and then it was over. An earthquake.

Mom, Eric, and Allison were at home when it happened. Allison, two years old, and Eric, three and a half years old, were watching TV in the downstairs family room. When the earthquake hit, they tried to climb up the stairs to find Mom while Mom worked her way down to find them. They all stumbled and then clung to each other throughout the remaining seconds. Mom's only thought was, *God, cover my other two children!* Dad was at the office holding onto desk lamps and covering his head. It was no small jolt either. That earthquake registered a 6.0 on the Richter scale. New cracks and fissures in the sidewalks and streets of Anchorage emerged from the rattling.

"Mom, what if there's another earthquake?" I felt squeaky, like a mouse. It was hard to verbalize the fear.

"God was with us the first time. Don't you think he'll be there the next time?"

The next time? I wanted her to relieve my fears, not confirm the likelihood of their being realized. I needed a practical assurance of safety, like, say, a safe room made of steel walls. My mother's quick reliance on an invisible God as our physical shield was hard for me to accept.

For the next several months, I walked like an old person, my head fixated on the cracks below my feet that might trip me up. Mom (who really could trip on a crack), on the other hand, seemed to walk tall and self-assuredly.

The whole earthquake experience fractured my peace of mind. I spent the rest of that year in Alaska on edge. I felt like someone perpetually waiting for the jack-in-the-box to spring out at me, whereas my mother and everyone else in our family seemed free of anxiety.

That said, at that point in my life, anxiety was not yet a constant companion; there were still days when I did not suffer its dreaded company. On one such freer occasion, the great beloved gospel singer and Billy Graham soloist, George Beverly Shea was scheduled to come to our house for dinner.

We were excited. My mother felt that part of her work with the BGEA was simply to be a hostess for such occasions. And she thought it would be nice if I helped, in some small way, to prepare the meal for that evening. She figured that I could handle rolling out biscuit dough. But as we worked, Mom got to telling me distracting stories about George Beverly Shea.

It turned out that my great-great-grandmother Ethel Rennick Marshall had grown up in Winchester, Ontario, with George Beverly Shea's family. While growing up in Winchester, Ethel and her family attended the church pastored by George Beverly Shea's father. Ethel's family and the Shea family were the two largest in the church, both with seven children.

One Sunday at church, George's grandfather, also a gifted singer, was providing special music. At one point, he opened his mouth so wide while singing that my great-great-grandfather turned to his wife, Ethel, and whispered, "If he opens his mouth any wider, he'll swallow that organ."

To this, Ethel quipped, "If he does, he'll pay for it." Mom chuckled as she told this punch line. Then she looked down to see that I had morphed the biscuit dough into dry, floury golf balls.

"Oh dear," she said. But it was too late by then. George Beverly Shea was on his way over. Mom cleaned up my mess, stuck the floury golf balls in the oven, and put on her warmest smile.

At dinner, George Beverly Shea howled with laughter at the same story Mom had told me earlier. He laughed till tears streamed down his face. Then Mom offered him a biscuit. "Would you care for a biscuit, Mr. Shea? Jessie helped make them." She tried to apologize with her eyes.

He popped the flour ball into his mouth. "Why, these are the best biscuits I've ever tasted!" He grinned at Mom. "In fact, I think I'll have another one." I smiled shyly and watched the beloved gospel singer graciously eat not one, not two, but four of my terrible biscuits.

When you move every year, it becomes very clear what objects you can and can't live without. For my mother, that essential thing was her Singer sewing machine. Every year the movers loaded it onto the truck, in its heavy plastic case, looking like a serious box of medical equipment.

Always baffling to me was that my mother, who was legally blind, could thread a needle in record time. Mom sewed every yard of rickrack on her children's Halloween costumes with that machine, not to mention many skirts and "fashionable" vests of the late 1980s. But in Alaska she got to use her sewing machine toward the adventurous life she hoped for.

Dad's work in preparation for the crusades put him in touch with a wide sampling of a city's cultural representatives. Keith Lowers, director of Youth for Christ, was the youth chairman for the crusade-organizing committee that year in Anchorage. Keith's son, Calvin, was an Iditarod dogsled racer. He raced his dogs on that harrowing journey from Anchorage to Nome.

Mom invited the Lowers over for dinner one night. Well into dessert and coffee, Calvin talked about his dogs: their personalities, their likes and dislikes, and their strengths and weaknesses when it came to being part of the team. By the evening's end, we Marshalls felt that we must meet these canine celebrities. Seeing our interest, Calvin turned to Mom and asked, "Becki, do you sew?"

She nodded brightly.

"Well, would you want to help sew some dog mittens?"

Calvin told her that his team of dogs wore mittens, or booties, while racing out there on the frozen tundra to protect the delicate pads of their feet. Every day of the race he changed their booties, which necessitated having a plentiful supply of them. He described for her the measurements of the soft cotton cloth and the Velcro strap that kept them in place.

Mom sewed twenty-eight pairs of sky blue mittens for Calvin's dogs as lovingly as if they were baby blankets. We got to be at the Iditarod starting line when the orange flag dropped and a hundred teams of gorgeous huskies leapt and tore at their harnesses like wild mustangs.

Months later, Calvin came over to our house again and presented Mom with one of the mittens she had made that his dog had worn in the race. We passed it around tenderly. It was as fragile as a Victorian doily, threadbare and beautiful. We smiled at the indentation of dog prints on the material. I could almost feel the frozen air and hear the dogs panting in rhythm.

Every year my mother shopped for groceries at a new, unfamiliar grocery store, squinting all over again for the sign above the cereal aisle. Every year she learned a whole new set of streets in our neighborhood. Every year she mapped out where the bus picked up her children for school and memorized the names of bus drivers, teachers, and principals. Every year she drove us to a new doctor for checkups. Every year she filled out those four pages of paperwork on the clipboard. Every year she unpacked her dishes, cups, and silverware and put them into new cupboards and drawers. She cooked us dinners in an unfamiliar kitchen. Like an absolving priest, she wiped clean the tables and the difficult days we passed as foreigners. She adjusted to make our transient life work.

CHAPTER 4

MY CRUSADE

I did write my father notes and hide them in his briefcase whenever I got the chance. The notes said things like, "When you are scared and sad, remember we are missing you!" This was mostly true, except when Mom took us for ice cream after dinner or to swim at a friend's pool. At those times, I forgot to miss Dad, which of course made me feel bad later—so I wrote him more notes to stymie the guilt.

I couldn't be sure, but I didn't sense that anyone else in my family worried about feeling guilty, or actually worried about anything.

I watched my older sister, Heather, like a hawk, wanting to emulate her charm. She smiled without showing her teeth; people thought her demure and intriguing. She was smooth and quiet and unruffled. Nothing seemed to bother her.

Compared to Heather, I was a golden retriever with its mouth open, always slightly whimpering in the back of the throat. I lived with a sensitive spirit that was nearly unbearable. It felt like walking into a force field that no one else could see. I was like one of those people who in the middle of conversation asks, "Does anybody else hear that buzzing sound?" My anxiety buzzed me. My father's fear of flying buzzed me. And the people in the highest seats of the stadium during Billy Graham's crusades buzzed me.

Though I never told a soul, I felt profoundly that it was my job to pray for those people near the highest rafters. It was my crusade, not because I chose it, but because I couldn't ignore it. My overly sensitive nature wouldn't let me dismiss them.

When the choir began to sing "Just As I Am," all my nerve endings tingled. I looked up into the shadowy top-tier seats and prayed for those people to hear God's calling. I felt they must have the most at stake, the most to lose. Why else would they stay on the edges of the crowd? I loved those strangers with abandon. They seemed like the outcast ones, the lost.

I prayed for these shadowy figures to find their way home, which was the same thing I prayed for myself. Even when very young, I sensed that to come forward to receive Christ led you one step closer to finding home. I wanted that for people who sat so far away. I wanted that for people like me who moved so far away.

When the choir sang, "Fightings within; fears without; just as I am, I come," I cried for all of us.

In 1988, on the second night of a crusade in Rochester, New York, Billy Graham gathered my family around him and asked the Lord to protect each of us throughout our moves and to bless us. Afterward, I nervously asked him, "Mr. Graham, will you write in my Bible, please?"

"Of course!" he boomed. I handed him the pen I'd brought along. He looked at me a moment, considering, and then he wrote.

I couldn't wait to read his inscription, but I held off looking at it until I got to my seat in the stadium later that evening. I opened up to the page he had signed and there read his short, direct note:

To Jessica, God bless you always.

—Billy Graham
Sept. 18, 1988

His handwriting was difficult to read, even for such a short inscription. Next to the "God bless you always" part was a reference to a verse. It looked to me like he'd written, "Psalm 18:11." I flipped through the Scriptures faster than a Talmud scholar to unearth this fortune cookie blessing from Billy Graham himself. Psalm 18:11 read, "He made darkness his covering, his canopy around him—the dark rain clouds of the sky."

My jaw dropped. I was baffled, and then I was horrified. What could it mean? This wasn't a blessing. Darkness? Rain clouds? I felt a mounting wave of anxiety rise up in me. In fact, the words sounded more like a curse. I sat for moment in trepidation. What was Billy Graham trying to tell me? Was I living under a canopy of sin? I wracked my brain. Two days prior I had stuck one of our hamsters down Allison's shirt, just to watch her shriek. And I might have lied just the teeniest bit to Mom and Dad about my score on a math test. Could Billy Graham sense all that? The worst part was that I had imagined that he and I were partners in ministry. Dad set the stage, Mr. Graham preached, and I prayed the lost souls near the rafters into the fold.

I took a harder look at the verse reference he'd written. His handwriting was chicken scratch. Perhaps the word wasn't *Psalms* after all. Clearly it started with a *P,* but maybe he'd written, "Proverbs." Back to page turning I went. I dug up Proverbs 18:11. It was bleak. "The wealth of the rich is their fortified city; they imagine it a wall too high to scale."

I sank down into my stadium seat. It was all suddenly obvious. Billy Graham believed I was doomed, and this was his way of telling me. I sat in total silence and anxiety for the rest of the service that night. At home, Mom tucked me into bed and said, "You were awfully quiet tonight. What's the matter?"

I burst into tears. "Billy Graham hates me." I heard her stifle a laugh, which only made me mad. "It's true. Look!" I thrust my Bible at her so she could see the inscription.

"Honey, I don't think that was the verse he was referring to. Your dad always tells me that Billy's handwriting is pretty awful. Let's see." With her bad eyes, but with a mother's determination, she stared down the numbers. "I don't think that's an eight. I think it says, 'Psalm 16:11.'"

It was too much to hope for. I buried my face in my pillow.

"Yep, that's the one. Listen, Jess. This is what Billy Graham wanted you to hear." I was just ten, so the full meaning of the verse was unclear to me. But when my mother read the right verse, I caught the tinkling, good sound of it, like wind chimes on the porch of a house up ahead, something not all mine but also calling my name, if I was willing to listen.

"You have made known to me the path of life; you will fill me with joy in your presence, with eternal joys at your right hand" (Psalms 16:11).

CHAPTER 5

SUCH A FINE WORD

Of my parents' four children, I struggled the most to reconcile myself to the transient life we lived for fifteen years.

Growing up in a Christian home, I knew that I should long for heaven one day, but of all the shoulds of Christianity, this was the one I wrestled with most. I was never very good at longing for a heavenly home, because I was too busy longing for an earthly one.

I had a hefty obsession with all things clerical as a child, and I had somewhere discovered order forms in triplicate. So I was delighted to find a big, thick pad of forms in my stocking one year. I thought of all the things I could list and organize—in triplicate.

That first layer was thin, white, and lined, begging to be filled. The middle layer was pink, and the bottom layer was a soft yellow. I adored the systemization of it. Nothing thrilled my heart more than to write up a pretend grocery list, give a copy to a (heavily disinterested) sibling, and file a copy in the shoe box under my bed where I kept very important papers. It seemed my entire life might just make sense if I could run it like an office.

There were so many messy details in my head that I didn't know how to organize, things like names and addresses of friends I'd made in each city, churches we attended, and teachers. Maybe all I needed to stave off anxiety were order forms in triplicate. I could keep my thoughts categorized that way. Better yet, I could keep my hopscotch, nomadic life organized that way.

I spent one whole evening listing on my triplicate forms all the addresses for houses where we had lived. I stood over Dad's shoulder as he read the newspaper after work, politely grilling him like a secretary, "What was the zip code for that neighborhood? And how do I spell that street name? City and state, please." By the end of the effort I was tired. And the list of addresses on my form didn't quite satisfy the longing in my heart.

My heart wanted *home* to fit neatly on those triplicate forms. It wanted *home* to be as easy as a grocery list, but home just wouldn't comply, wouldn't be pinned down so readily.

Therefore, by the time I was ten, I was convinced that *home* must mean the very thing I could not have: it meant staying put.

Home meant knowing a house so well you could walk its halls with your eyes closed. Every creek and floorboard: a physical memory. Home meant knowing which room you had entered simply by its unique hum of silence. Home was living three blocks away from the house where you were born or had grown up. It meant that your grandmother lived ten minutes away and so did a smattering of cousins.

You could ride your bike over to your cousins' house after school. Your grouchy, run-down aunt would be folding laundry from the line and manage a limp wave as you knocked down your kickstand. You might stay an hour and pick up with the Monopoly game you and your cousins had started last week. Or you might not. You might get in a fight with your cousins about what to watch on TV. The point was that your coming over was no big deal. It was routine. It was predictable and free of anxiety.

Home also meant a whole lot of non sequitur information about your hometown. "That right there is where my uncle's car dealership used to be. Now it's a Best Buy."

I longed to offhandedly remark on how a landscape had changed, how a town had changed year after year. I envied people's yawns of boredom about their own hometown, their ability to stand at a bus stop and casually remark, "Wow, the snow is really coming down a lot sooner this year." Home meant knowing and never leaving a place and its people. It meant everyday banality.

Home meant ordinary stuff, and ordinary was not my life.

By contrast, I had never once lived in a town for more than a year. I knew nothing about how any neighborhood had changed. When my family arrived in a city, it was for one inning or like a celebrity cameo appearance on a TV sitcom. The live audience cheers and whistles when the celebrity enters stage left, and cheers and whistles again after she exits. The Marshalls made one cameo appearance and then vanished.

We were in town for one cycle of seasons—fall, winter, spring, and summer— and then we were gone, getting waved to and whistled at by newly hatched friends as we drove out of sight. My father's work with Billy Graham allowed us one year, which isn't even long enough for dust to settle on boxes in the attic.

It was in Rochester, New York, our eighth move with the BGEA, that I met some people who had gotten the memo about home. Four families who seemed to comprehend my personal definition of the word. They had all grown up out of the flat, right-angled streets of Rochester, New York, and had married their high school sweethearts and were raising families a stone's throw away from each other. Amazingly, they opened their arms to my family. At first, their warmth felt like an awkward embrace from unfamiliar relatives. But these families possessed an enticing sense of community and, kindly enough, offered it to us.

They were the Adams, the Kadars, the Kings, and the Knapps. They all had kids around the same ages as Heather, Eric, Allison and myself. Mom and Dad had met the Kings at a local church, and they all hit it off immediately. When Mom mentioned we were living on Dellwood Drive, they said, "Oh, some of our best friends, the Kadars, live on that street."

I don't remember ever being introduced to the Kadar boys, but I can clearly recall the heat of our authentic childhood play by October of that year. The Kadars had three raucous boys. The oldest, Zach, became Eric's buddy. Zach, Eric, and I rode our bikes together to school every day. After a few weeks, Zach invited us to ride to his grandmother's house (his "gummy") and have cookies there after school. He said his cousins might be there too. Zach was living my dream of *home*.

With the Kadar boys, we played every kind of street game we could think of when parents wouldn't let us in either house. And when it snowed, the Kadar boys, Eric, Allison, and I built forts and traps and bombed each other with cruel ice balls. We competed fiercely in everything and fought over each other's toys without shame.

The Kadars owned a Nintendo system. We did not. So Eric, Allison, and I sprinted for the Kadars' house nearly every afternoon after school. I can only imagine the looks that passed between Patty and Bill Kadar on evenings when he slumped through their door after a long day at the Kodak plant. There again were the loud Billy Graham brats, arguing over Nintendo controllers, grinding cheese puffs into the carpet.

Eric and I often pitted ourselves in knock-down, drag-out verbal battles against the Kadar brothers. We threw blame like pebbles from the nearby creek when one of our bikes seemed bent out of shape or our package of snappers went missing. It was volatile and real; it was the closest we Marshall kids had ever come to genuine community, and we loved it.

On one particular occasion, our relationship with the Kadars and that authentic friendship we were building, demanded to be tested. Zach had spent the night at our house (a fact that should have tipped off our mothers). After a sleepover, we needed breathing room in order to like each other again, but both moms wanted some distance from their kids, so we fought and played the next day too.

Mom had a visitor over from church. "Go play outside, or go the Kadars' house if Mrs. Kadar will let you."

It was dreary outside and we had already been to the creek the day before, so we wandered over to the Kadars' house, bored and restless, a precise recipe for damage. Patty Kadar was busy trying to get her downstairs clean, so she banished us to the bedrooms. Zach's room was across from the one Ben and Nate shared. We started our Lego play in Zach's room, but a hot discrepancy over a Lego man's head (they were always popping off, getting lost like Barbie shoes) led to shouting, then to division.

Nate, Ben, and Zach ran into the other bedroom clutching the Lego head, cackling in triumph from behind the door. Eric and I looked at one another and stiffened. Downstairs, Patty vacuumed.

Blazing with vindication, Eric and I ran head-on and full steam at Ben and Nate's door. We hit it hard, like baby elephants. When it didn't budge the first time, we braced our shoulders to give it another bang. The laughter on the other side ceased. Ben and Nate called us some awful names, and our reply was one more fierce blow at the door. This time the door cried out. Off it sprung from its hinges and fell into the boys on the other side. We all screamed in shock and secret thrill at our own devastating power. By then Patty had finished vacuuming.

In all my young life, I had never witnessed a mom finally come off her own hinges. She grabbed Eric and me by our sweaty T-shirts. The decent Christian housewife was finished being hospitable to the Billy Graham brats.

I wanted to get out of the Kadars' house fast, but Mrs. Kadar had put me and Eric in a kind of WrestleMania hold. She dragged us like mutts out to our bikes. We rode home in guilty silence. We knew Mom would be mortified, and we couldn't possibly escape her finding out. She read our white faces immediately. "What did you do?" she demanded.

I blurted it all out—but I made sure to explain that Eric had started it. Mom went silent, the kind of silence in moms that precedes a flurry of terrifying action. Moments later, she dragged us by our now seriously stretched-out collars down the street to apologize. Knowing we would face more of Patty's wrath seemed like punishment enough. But something remarkable had happened while we were gone.

Patty was crying when we arrived. Her face was in her hands as she sat on her front stoop. Zach, Ben, and Nate were very quiet, guilty by association, probably still up in the doorless room. When she saw us, Patty opened her arms and locked me and Eric in an embrace.

"I'm so sorry for yelling at you. That was so uncalled for. Would you forgive me?" She looked up at Mom; both their eyes wet.

Mom and Dad made Eric and me pay for new door hinges with our allowance money. Plus, we had to write a formal apology letter to the whole Kadar family for being slightly less than Christlike.

That day with the Kadars was the first time in my life that friendship felt more like family. I didn't have cousins who lived down the street to argue with. I wasn't so lucky. But suddenly I had friends filling in the gaps. It was like a taste of real home. I wanted more of it.

Out of the fifteen years my family hopscotched the globe with the BGEA, just once I got my wish to stay put for longer than a year. Billy Graham decided to hold a crusade in Rochester in 1987, and then in Montreal in 1989—and in between them would be a London crusade. Instead of transplanting his family to London for a year, Dad had us stay in Rochester right there down the street from the Kadars while he made the grueling commute, week after week, between countries. This sacrifice on his part was lost on me as a child, but the marvel of living in the same city for two years in a row was not.

I would get to attend the same school with my friends, to live in the same house, to experience again and again all my bike routes and happy corners. Come the first day of school, I could swagger past my old classroom, rolling my eyes at the new batch of fourth graders—so young! I could creep into the girls' bathroom's last stall and find my love inscription to Adam Jones, the boy I'd loved *last* year.

During our second year in Rochester, Mom and Dad caved and bought us pet rabbits. Heather and I tried to believe they were like dogs, taking them for walks on leashes, which resulted in some runaway attempts.

On more than one wintry night, Dad and Mr. Kadar combed the neighborhood with flashlights, thrusting the beams into dark shrubbery. Twice we lost the rabbits and twice the dads found them and brought them home, much to our hearts' delight.

Our family slept deeply, like bears, that second year—warm, safe, and surrendered to our (rented) den. Two years in the same city: we had gotten away with something. Somewhere in the family subconscious was the truth, that we were going to have to leave this home and our friends, but we put that reality off for as long as possible. Instead, we pulled the blankets up around our necks and relished a sense of familiarity for one free year.

When finally we did say good-bye to the Kadars, the Adams, the Kings, and the Knapps, it was as serious as a heartbreak. As a family, we tried to pull that Band-Aid off fast, but our friends wouldn't stand for it. Apparently they wanted to feel their loss. We were forced to as well. There were good-bye parties and toasts, last sleepovers for us kids, and countless good-bye hugs. It was torture.

Our dreaded departure day arrived in July. As we drove away from our house on Dellwood Drive, something seemed to claw at my chest. My heart felt ripped and torn. It was like holding our rabbits. When they felt unsafe, if your grip was off, they clawed at your chest, their pupils dilated and their eyes scared. Their claws opened full against your shirt as their back legs pummeled for footing. I was a wild and terrified rabbit, once again without friends or a home.

My eyes glistened with tears. I craned my neck to see the house we had called home for two whole years. We turned down Dellwood Drive and moved out of Rochester, New York, forever.

I wondered if I'd ever find my footing again.

I wished to consume the houses we chose every year. I wished to make them mine, to own them, to pin them to a spreading board like beautifully preserved insects. We called them *home*—we called them ours—but there was no loyalty there. Yes, we slept inside their four walls and stacked our cups inside their cupboards. We played games of catch in the backyard. These things we did. But in the end we always betrayed the meaning of the word *home*.

We left, like an unfaithful spouse.

I wanted to exhaust the walls of a house, to live somewhere so long that rebuilding was necessary. I wanted to wear out the paint in my bedroom, to remodel the room and grow inside it, grow as big as Alice, and then pocket with affection the house that had held me.

Either we know a place all the way— build and plant from the ground on which we stand—or we forget this place ever happened. Our lifestyle with the Billy Graham Evangelistic Association seemed to insist on the latter.

I grieved my family's betrayal of such a fine word as *home*.

CHAPTER 6

PANIC

In 1984, we moved to Hartford, Connecticut. Dad found us a duplex home in Glastonbury, a town of thirty thousand people along the banks of the Connecticut River, south of Hartford. It was a place of dense forests, Thoreau-type woods, which had the kind of meaty trees that could be chopped down and turned into a sturdy cabin in days. You could hack away and never put a dent in the air quality, never leave a bald spot worth speaking of. There were maple, pine, and swaying whitewashed birch—and not a foot between them. It seemed to me they massed and huddled together like a thick, impenetrable line in Red Rover.

But those soldiering, noble trees in our New England neighborhood took a severe beating in 1984 when Hurricane Gloria hit. The winds whipped and forced trees to lie prostrate. As a family, we watched the destruction from the sliding glass window in our living room. I saw the havoc from safety, but my child's heart was timorous. The wind showed no mercy. All the roots were unearthed, and the trees died. How could I ensure that this wouldn't happen to me? In the days following the hurricane, we could barely walk down the sidewalk. Dead trees blocked our way. Sometimes I gripped my mother's hand so hard that she said, "Ouch, Jess," and pulled it away. What if my family—my roots in a shifting, transient life—pulled away?

36

It was as if the storm outside had laid siege to my mind. I began to have nightmares about being left behind by my family in our moves with Billy Graham. I feared that Mom and Dad had a plan to get to that elusive sense of home I dreamed of and weren't planning on taking me along. I was dead weight, cumbersome baggage. I'd seen what they did with stuff that didn't fit into packing boxes. It was given away or was tossed to the curb. And if they left me, how would I find my way home? I didn't know where it was, let alone how to get there.

Time and time again, my parents tried to assure me that I was loved and accepted, but as a child I doubted there was a grand design for good in my life.

One day, my swelling fears about home and abandonment spilled over from nighttime into the shocking light. I experienced the first of many panic attacks to come. That year in Hartford, Mom and Dad had enrolled me and Heather in gymnastic classes. One day after class, Heather went home with a friend. On the drive home in the car, Mom said to me, "I need to stop at the CVS and get a few things." Eric, five years old, and Allison, three years old, were in the backseat.

"Stay right here with them, Jess. I'll be right back." She hopped out of the car and walked briskly through the parking lot and into the store. With round rabbit eyes, I watched her go. *What if she never comes back?*

With that one nuclear thought, my sense of security toppled like a tree in a storm. And the crash upended my roots. I whipped my head around. There were Eric and Allison sitting contentedly. They trusted that Mom would be back for them. But the fear of abandonment rose in my chest, growing stronger and stronger until I couldn't breathe. I had to get out of the car.

I clawed at the door handle. Once outside, I began to scream. I could hear myself screaming in a sort of underwater way. Then I began to shake, choking for air. Coming toward me was a woman with grocery bags in her hands, headed to her car. I rushed her in my panic. "Help me. Help me find my mom!" She blinked and then only stared. I grabbed her arms. "Please, help me find my mom!"

I was desperate, capable of anything in my state of panic. The woman pried my arms off and nearly sprinted away to her car. I couldn't understand. I stood there shaking to the bone, gulping for air, crazed with the terror that my mother had abandoned me, longing for someone who would help me find my mother or, better yet, wishing someone would knock me out of my misery.

Of course Mom came back. In her mind, she had never left. And the mental state she found me in upon her return became a source of misunderstanding between us for most of my childhood. She was horrified and hurt that I imagined she would abandon her child. I was horrified and hurt that she couldn't conceive of my fear. She thought me dramatic and over-reactionary. I found her flippant and insensitive.

From that point on, panic attacks ravaged me—laid waste to me like the wind and the rain. I knew no one else who suffered them. I thought that the feeling that I would die from fear was the terrible hack job of God's wiring in my brain. Simply living became that old game of Operation. I had to take the utmost care to avoid the dangerous edge of thought, or else I would get zapped with a panic attack. And the most hazardous thought continued to be, *What if my family leaves me. How will I find my way home?* But avoiding a zap was very hard when everything about my life was so unsteady, so very unstable.

During the weeks following my first panic attack in Hartford, I trembled with aftershock. It was like the serious earthquake we'd experienced in Alaska. For days after it, the earth still shook with tremors. All was not at rest underground.

Neither was my mind at rest. Mom and Dad were at a loss for how to help me. I was only seven years old and hadn't the terminology to describe my anxiety. I couldn't sleep for fear of another panic attack.

Long after my siblings were asleep, I got out of bed. Downstairs, my parents were trying to enjoy a few quiet hours together in front of the television before their day ended. I cried on Dad's arm. I couldn't explain or unpack my fear of abandonment, my feeling of being homeless. He and Mom prayed with me, which was good, but not an immediate cure. It would take time for their prayers to take root.

So I asked for music.

Dad owned a Marantz turntable with quadraphonic speakers and headphones. It was hooked up in the living room area. In those late hours of the night, he laid me—with skinny legs and wearing just a nightshirt—down on the couch and put the massive headphones on me. I wanted to hear "the one in the sunglasses." Dad knew what I meant—Bob Dylan's *Blood on the Tracks* album. Specifically, I liked "Shelter from the Storm." I rubbed my dry feet together and held my hands over the headphones as the song began.

I listened hard as a means of distraction from circling fear. Dylan wasn't hurried or panicked. He was just singing a song. I could sing along too—and I did.

It was a five-minute reprieve from anxiety. The sound of his guitar pacified me. He knew how to play it and make it drive his story along. I didn't understand the details of the song, but the chorus was all I needed. "I'll give you shelter from the storm" felt like a promise. It echoed what I had been told that God could do for me. The song felt tight and secure against my heart like a seat belt. It was a good feeling for a girl who felt pitched about.

CHAPTER 7

TRAVELING WITH THE
BEATLES AND BOB DYLAN

In the Marshall family, we talked about God and Jesus in the same way we talked about the Beatles and Bob Dylan. We praised their good works and how they transformed us, and then we told people about it. This was evangelism, as I understood it.

My father and mother felt that Billy Graham understood the beautiful simplicity of sharing what changed you. After we lived in a city for several months, Mom and Dad said to neighbors, "Come hear Billy Graham tell the story of Jesus," in the same way they said, "Listen to this song, kids."

As I saw it, the Beatles and Bob Dylan had everything to do with my family's faith-centered life and ministry, and I had good evidence to support this unlikely fusion.

I had grown up hearing exactly who my father had been before I was born—before he was *reborn* in Christ: an experimental, lost youth in love with a band of four gents from England. Before Dad ever became a Christian and even before he saw the music soar from the speakers in his dorm room that fateful night, he expressed his passion for the Beatles in the form of a wooden record-holding crate.

It was a basic plank-board box he'd found at a hardware store near his university. He had taken it home to Warren, Michigan, on a summer break. When the inspiration hit him, he went to work. First he stained the box, and then he sketched with pencil the detailed images of all four members of the Beatles into its siding. When he felt he'd captured their likenesses, he burned their impressions into the wood and then delicately painted each one.

The results were impressive. On every surface of the crate were detailed renderings of John Lennon, Paul McCartney, George Harrison, and Ringo Starr. Dad even painted the famed yellow submarine along with an image of John. John's comment bubble read, "All our friends are all aboard! Many more of them live next door." Dad had taken the transformed crate back to college with him the next fall, and his roommate and suite mates adored it. It became the album box, a suitable nest for their beloved music.

And then, five years later, my father and mother had a child, and later three more. The album box quickly slipped from its high post; it became the toy box.

We owned a set of wooden blocks, the old kind that could really do some damage if one clocked you in the head. The four of us children used those blocks in every kind of imaginative play. They could be the frame of a Barbie house or, if lined up one after another, the dividing line between your stuff and mine. They were essential for fort building—three stacked on top of each other held down a corner of a fort nicely. And we kept those multipurpose blocks in the Beatles wooden crate.

Every time I pulled out a block from the crate, I glanced again at the pictures my father had etched into the siding. The colors were still bright after many years and many nicks and bumps on moving trucks.

The Beatles were there with us while we played make-believe, when we imagined ourselves into fairy tales or Bible stories. The Fab Four were burned into the wood and into my psyche and into the fabric of our days, no matter where we lived. They were as tangible as wooden blocks and as mystical as God the Father.

The Beatles toy box traveled everywhere with us, and so did our LPs and cassette tapes of their music. Some things got lost in the moves, like library books. Others got left behind on purpose, like disagreeable pets. But there was always room for the music, which we never left behind.

The Beakins Moving Company packed our big, worldly belongings and headed out like the first scout in a wagon train. We followed behind. If we were moving somewhere stateside, our family often traveled the long distances between moves in a BGEA industrial cargo van. These cargo vans were dirt brown with small windows. It seemed they'd never seen a carwash. (As teenagers, my siblings and I were terribly embarrassed by these vehicles. In high school, my friends used to see one parked in our driveway and call out, "Hey, Marshall, the eighties called. The A-Team wants their van back!")

The BGEA cargo vans supplied seating for eight, with two long, springy seats in the middle and two bucket seats up front for pilot and copilot. Included was the essential tape deck on the console.

The very back of the van was usually rather empty, since the Beakins' truck carried all of our belongings. If Dad was in a good mood before we headed out of town, he could sometimes be persuaded to make a kind of sleeping fort for one of us kids in the way back of the van. He'd layer down some blankets and toss in a few fluffy pillows, creating just enough room for a child's squirmy legs to stretch out. This sleeping fort became the coveted spot in the van, second only to shotgun position.

To secure your spot in the fort, you either had to ask very politely if it were in fact your turn or you had to be the most obnoxious child in the van—hitting, kicking, begging for fast food and candy. The second approach got you your wish, but it came as more of a banishment from Dad: "To the back of the van!" Naturally, I tended toward the second approach.

It was in my banishment at the rear of the van that I fell in love with my father's favorite music. The back speaker cages were level with the sleeping fort. I could press my ear on them and glide into the music, hour after hour, on the road. It was as close to personally knowing the Beatles and Bob Dylan as a girl could get.

The music took all of my broken stuff—panic attacks, fledgling friendships, unfinished conversations, and unmet expectations of a new town—and corralled it all into melody. The music was a set of big capable hands, fashioning goodness and meaning in the parts of my life that didn't make sense, the parts that caused me unhinging anxiety. The music said that even the aching stressors of our transient life were redeemable. The music promised me, better than a bedside kiss from a parent, that I would find my way home.

There was the first track on *Sgt. Pepper's Lonely Hearts Club Band*: the sound of an arena filling, the parts of a show all juicing up, the elements coming together. I knew this sound entirely; it was the same cacophony I heard before every Billy Graham crusade.

Dad liked to sing along to "Getting Better." The only time I ever heard him sing falsetto was to that first verse. He tapped the steering wheel in rhythm as the song started. "I used to get mad at my school. The teachers who taught me weren't cool," he sang. As I listened, I thought about a photograph of him that I'd seen in one of our family albums: Dad at college in ripped bell-bottoms while yelling at a cop, his finger in the cop's face, lit with disgust for The Man.

Then there were songs like "Being for the Benefit of Mr. Kite!" which caused me real concern. The cadence made me tingle with dread. It captured the mental instability I felt with every panic attack I experienced.

I also wrung out of the Beatles' music every drop of comedy. I marked the nonsensical—the Beckett-like absurdity—in it, and I hid this in my pocket like a secret note to pass to myself when I needed a laugh. When I sat all alone at lunch at another new school, the music was my companion.

I liked to hold the cassette case for the *Sgt. Pepper* album. Who were all those faces? A few of them I recognized: Marilyn Monroe, about whom my parents had told me, and, of course, Bob Dylan. His face in the crowd didn't seem random to me at all. I imagined my family in the neon marching band costumes. I imagined Dad, with his arm around a cardboard cutout of Billy Graham, propped up next to figurines of the Beatles and Bob Dylan, and the cloud of witnesses behind him would be Jesus and all the friends our family had said good-bye to on our journey with Billy Graham. This was a family photograph of the real and the mythic in my life.

In addition, I felt profoundly that I knew Bob Dylan through the music on the *Slow Train Coming* and *Saved* albums, the same way I knew Billy Graham when the choir sang "Just as I Am" every night of every crusade. The message in these two albums was the same one that my parents taught us at home while praying and reading *The Picture Bible* with us in our beds at night. "He knows your needs even before you ask," or "You gotta serve somebody." I knew my parents desired to serve God only. Bob Dylan didn't apologize for it, so his songs gave me courage.

With every track of music, I renewed my faith in the free-falling way we lived, and I forgave my father silently for it there in the back of the van.

Sometimes, as we listened to Bob Dylan on those road trips, Dad could be persuaded to tell a favorite family story.

Just months after Dad began to work for Billy Graham, he was asked to help out the BGEA team at the Baltimore, Maryland, crusades, which were held at the old Memorial Stadium in June of 1981. On one of the crusade nights in Baltimore, Dad stood on the stadium floor in his pressed khakis and blue blazer. He had a confident stance that made him look to be in charge.

A man approached Dad and whispered in his ear, "I'm Bob Dylan's manager. He's here tonight. I just wanted to let someone official know." That was all he said. There was my young father, a child of the sixties, a war-protesting student of the seventies, and a Christian for all of eight years. There was hardly a figure more iconic in Dad's journey toward God than Bob Dylan. He could barely get the words out, "Show me."

The man walked Dad toward the seats directly above home plate and pointed six rows deep. There he was, if you thought to look. Like a cardboard cutout of himself, in telltale Bob Dylan sunglasses but with a ball cap low, keeping his shoulders hunched. Unawares, people sat all around. Dad stared for a long moment, imagining a meeting between Bob Dylan and Billy Graham.

One year prior, Dylan had released *Saved,* and before that *Slow Train Coming,* baffling people the world over with vulnerable songs about faith in Christ. Dad considered how a meeting with Billy Graham might encourage this most misunderstood and scrutinized face of American music. He fumbled for words. "I'll see what I can do."

Dad went up the chain of command. First he sought Charlie Riggs. "Billy Graham has no time for that," Riggs said dismissively.

Then Dad went to Don Bailey, head of PR. "Billy is too busy to meet with that guy."

Finally my dad approached T. W. Wilson, Mr. Graham's personal assistant. It took a lot of courage for Dad to address him. T. W. Wilson's only response was, "Why would Billy Graham want to meet Bob Dylan?"

If it needed explaining, Dad knew he had lost.

The chasm at that time between the old men of the BGEA, who feared the world and hovered around Mr. Graham, and the newly converted—the artist or revolutionary thinker—was too vast.

Many years later, when my father had the ear and friendship of the man himself, he told Billy about this story. Mr. Graham was shocked. "Why did T. W. tell you that? Of course I would have met with Bob Dylan!"

I understood the story about Bob Dylan, so I looked for him at crusades. And I prayed for the ones who were like him, hiding behind sunglasses, misunderstood, and marginalized. They were my shadowed friends in the highest bleacher seats.

Dad's Bob Dylan story said opportunity missed, which wasn't good, but it could be the thorn that he vowed to loosen or the reason to have his hook ready for the next time. My father wouldn't let a chance like that get away from him again. The story said that he wouldn't. The next time he had the chance, he would seize it. The next time a music man came his way, he would orchestrate a beautiful convergence.

Billy Graham prays with the Marshall family (Archer, center) in Rochester, NY, September, 1988.

September, 1988 (clockwise: Heather, Becki, Jess, Allison, Eric, Rick Marshall)

Billy Graham prays after giving the invitation for people to receive Jesus Christ as their Savior.

PRESS FOCUS

SECOND SECTION OF COUNTY PRESS, HAVERFORD PRESS, DREXEL HILL PRESS AND SPRINGFIELD PRESS

Wednesday, June 17, 1992

Delco Ready For Billy Graham's Visit To The Vet

Billy Graham

The Marshalls, who have been around the world with the Billy Graham Association, now live in Newtown Square. They are (back) Becki, Heather and Rick; and Allison, Jessica and Eric. With them is Ceilidh who was obtained in Scotland, Rick's last assignment with Billy Graham Association. They plan to remain at their home for another year while Rick works on the Pittsburgh crusade.

Photo by Jane Gallaway

48

*Rick (Archer's father) discusses last minute details
with Billy Graham before he preaches.*

*The first Youth Night, orchestrated by Archer's father, Rick. June
11, 1994. (seated, DC Talk, Michael W. Smith and band.)*

CHAPTER 8

QUILTED COLOR-BLOCK SQUARES

By the time I was eleven years old, the prospects for getting my definition of *home* were looking grim. I had lived in eight different cities before I had even hit puberty, including Paris, Fargo, and Anchorage—and not one of them for longer than two years. I had culture, language, and experience, but I didn't have a home that I never had to leave.

Billy Graham continued to rely heavily on my father for the preparation and direction of his evangelistic crusades; therefore, our family, much to my dismay, continued a nomadic lifestyle. We moved to a city in late August and stayed until late June, just after the week when the Billy Graham crusades concluded. And then we were off again.

But there were two untethered months in between the place we left and the place we were going. Those were July and August. And for our family, there was an enormous need for rest in between moves. We needed to rest from the adrenalized, onward-ho mentality of our lives. We found our respite during summer months on the shores of Lake Michigan.

It was my mother's parents, affectionately known as Grammy and Papa, who lived in the sleepy town of Bridgman in southwest Michigan, just a five-minute drive from lush and quiet Weko Beach.

Grammy and Papa lived in a split-level in Bridgman. The train tracks were five hundred yards down the road from their house, and so was Red Arrow Highway. There were no neighbors to the right of them, just brambling blackberry bushes and a half mile of weeds. Papa was the pastor at Woodland Shores Baptist Church.

There was virtually zero entertainment or culture in Bridgman. If you wanted to see a movie, you needed to drive to St. Joseph. If you wanted to go clothes shopping, you should drive to South Bend, in the next state. But my siblings and I wanted none of those things. We only wanted our cousins and grandparents, their overly air-conditioned house on Vista Drive, and the mild waters of Lake Michigan in July.

We drove to Bridgman every June in one of the ugly BGEA cargo vans. It was usually a long trip, depending on where we were living at the time. With every mile, our anticipation grew. We knew exactly what to expect when we arrived at Grammy and Papa's, and that's why we loved it.

By the time we were on Baldwin Road, two miles from their house, my seat belt was off and my heart was pounding in my chest. It seemed like a miracle that we had made it back to Bridgman again. I felt like a soldier returning home after so many tours. We had gotten away with something big.

I looked around at my siblings and parents, who were in the van with me. We had all survived another gut-wrenching year of being the new folks in town, another year of navigating a city we didn't know, another year of steering our way through new social circles, and another Billy Graham crusade on the books for Dad. The mercy that we had all survived these challenges burned at the corners of my eyes.

Baldwin was a long road, agonizingly long. We strained our eyes for the faded Donna Drive sign on the left. Grammy and Papa lived on Vista Drive, which curled around into the end of Donna. When you turned down Donna Drive, you could see my grandparents' house at the very end of the road, a quarter of a mile away.

But that was too far.

One year, when the four of us kids were under the age of ten, our anticipation for Grammy's house burst its seams. "Can we run to the house?" we begged, bouncing up and down on the springy pleather seats.

Mom and Dad laughed, "Fine, go ahead. Watch for cars!" Dad pulled over to the side of the road, just at the entrance of Donna Drive, and four kids, all arms and legs, tumbled out like monkeys. And run, we did, the entire quarter of a mile down Donna Drive and straight up to our grandparents' house.

The sprint to the house seemed the right way to express my feelings. My legs and arms pumped, my heart heaved as I tore for my grandparents' home. It was good to exhaust myself in the pursuit of the people and place that I was coming to love most. Grammy and Papa were waiting, and I wouldn't delay. Something so good seemed to require my physicality.

Finally, I reached the house. It hadn't moved. It stood like a sentry at its post: faithful, resolute, ready to shield me again. The two windows on the second floor facing the street looked like eyes to me, always open, always watching and waiting for our return. I heard the soft kissing sound of the front door's weather stripping and knew my grandparents had come outside to welcome us back. Every summer, from that point on, at least one of us, Heather, Eric, Allison, or I, would run the length of Donna Drive that first day we returned to Bridgman.

Each summer it was the same thing. Grammy tried to get us Marshall grandkids interested in making friends with kids from Woodland Shores Church. She figured that all children wanted to make new friendships, but she was forgetting that that was the work we four kids did every single school year of our lives. Heather, Eric, Allison and I were virtually friendship salespeople in each new city—walking up to neighbor kids or seating ourselves next to total strangers in the cafeteria. "Making friends" sounded like our nine-to-five jobs, and we were on summer vacation, thank you very much.

The only relationships we had any interest in cultivating come summers in Bridgman were those with our cousins. And we had a lot of them in Michigan. They flooded Grammy's house when word got out that the Marshalls were back from another year of traveling with Billy Graham. My mom was one of five. All her siblings and their kids crammed in at Grammy's to spend time with us again. Nothing made me happier than a reunion with my cousins.

Behind Grammy's house was a creek, sometimes very dry and sometimes turbulent with warm water life. Come summertime, it was a perfect breeding ground for giant frogs. And my cousins and I loved to catch frogs.

Whenever Grammy had us doing some tedious job like shucking corn or hanging beach towels on the line, the frogs croaked and taunted us. We'd moan with frog lust and shout to each other, "Get a bucket!" and "Where's the net?" Flushed from our beach sunburns, we'd run to the creek's edge. Why had we squandered the day? We stood frozen on the creek bank, barely breathing lest we scare the frogs into the reeds.

I wanted those frogs in a bucket to gawk at and tease, but more often than not I let my brother and favorite cousin, Jeff, do the catching. Instead I stood on the banks and barked orders at them: "To the left, over there! You're doing it wrong!"

Eric and Jeff bore daggers at me with their eyes and spit whispers. "Shut up! You'll scare them away!"

We wanted the praises of our aunts and uncles. We wanted to oust them from Grammy's kitchen, and have them peer down into our bucket o' frogs and praise us: "Wow, that's a big one there. Who caught that one?"

Though the spoils were grand, Grammy's creek proved less than ideal for frogging, as the creek banks were steep and the mosquitos nearly unbearable. But there was another frogging spot. Down

Baldwin Road was a small retirement community with a gorgeous pond, sunning itself brightly. It was flat, reedy at the edges, and shallow in the middle—and easily accessible. Any kid with frogs on the brain could see that it was ideal. The one small problem was that it was private land.

Mom and Aunt Darlene made it sound like the retired people who lived there sat on their tiny porches with sticks and fireplace pokers in hand, ready to beat small children who dared trespass their lush pond, who dared get enjoyment off their landscaping fees.

One boring, overcast day, Jeff, Eric, and I couldn't stand it anymore. We wanted to go frogging at the Baldwin Road pond in a bad way. Our mothers shook their heads in firm resistance. No amount of begging would convince them.

"Let's make petition signs; that will get their attention." Jeff was into politics. He was class president at his school. He seemed to think this was the best means to get what we wanted.

"We'll march up and down the driveway with our signs."

It sounded obnoxious but smart. Eric and I nodded. We scrounged up some paper and the broomsticks from Grammy's garage, some tape from Papa's desk, and a big fat marker from my craft supplies. After a time of thoughtful deliberation, we concurred on our slogan, "Kids for Frogs!"—as if our aim had anything to do with amphibian conservation.

Half of our plan worked. We got our parents' attention. Our mothers howled with laughter at our signs till their mascara ran. We marched out on the driveway for an entire afternoon, long after our mothers had gone back inside to help Grammy with dinner. We never did get permission to go frogging at the retirement home pond, and though we'd never admit it, we didn't have the guts to face old people with dirty teeth and whacking sticks.

If we weren't dreaming of frogs in a bucket, my siblings and cousins and I wanted to go to Weko Beach. It was the first thing we asked for in the morning, after our third bowl of Fruit Loops.

"Grammy, will you drive us to the beach today?" Her gracious yeses worked on me like the overflowing cup in Scripture.

Every day she packed us a cooler of food, after which we'd all pile into cars, tightly seated next to aunts in bathing suits with soft, fleshy thighs. We drove past the Dairy Queen on the main street, past the thrift store whose sign always read "CLOSED," and down toward the thick green trees. It was Bridgman's only boast: a beautiful, quiet stretch of beach.

Because of the lake effect weather, the soft white sand piled itself in curvaceous dunes a hundred feet back from the shore. The lake water by late July was an easy seventy-five degrees. The dunes were incredible for hiking up and then running down, straight into the water. They were so steep that it became a contest of keeping up with your own speed. You had to focus all your attention on churning your legs, or else you'd fall with a whirl into sand.

We children dug massive holes and buried each other. We built sandcastles and wrote our names as big as we could along the beach, afterward watching the waves wash them away. My cousins and I swam to the farthest buoy until the lifeguard whistled us back in. And then we threw our spent bodies down onto Grammy's beach quilts, our chests heaving, our eyes burning. Mom and the aunts handed us ham sandwiches and Fresca. We gulped it all down and then went back out for more.

We only left the beach when the sunlight danced on the water in that certain four-o'-clock way. At that point, one of the aunts would say, "Grammy'll want help with dinner. Time to go." I never wanted to leave that beach. It was the one place I never lived, but it was the only place that felt like home.

Once, after our year in Paris, France, Dad secretly planned a family vacation for us in the Bahamas in conjunction with a work trip. In 1983, Mr. Graham had received the Templeton Prize for progress in religion. The prize would be formally proffered by Price Philip in London. A precondition of the prize was that the recipient go down to the Bahamas and give a speech. So, the Billy Graham

Evangelistic Association agreed to hold an evangelical meeting in Nassau, and Dad worked on the preparations.

During our year in Paris, Dad jet-setted every couple of months, swimming trunks and snorkel mask in briefcase, down to the Bahamas for some island-style, grueling prep work. While there, he met a vivacious guy named Donald Maura, who was part owner of Maura Lumber and Marine Co. in Nassau. Donny had signed up to be on the BGEA committee for the Nassau Mission. He became an invaluable resource and friend to Dad.

Donny and his bubbly wife, Barbara, owned a tropical-paradise home on the bay with their two tanned, always barefoot kids, David and Jeanie. They insisted on meeting Dad's family.

At the airport in Paris, Dad made the announcement, "Instead of going straight to Grammy and Papa's, we're going to the Bahamas!"

Allison's lip quivered. "I don't want to! I want to go to Grammy's house!"

"What's the Bahamas?" Eric blurted. I felt the same frustration. Allison and Eric began crying. We didn't want the Bahamas. We wanted Michigan. Dad and Mom stared wide-eyed at their kids. They hadn't realized that Bridgman had become our only shred of predictability.

I was the most at peace at my grandparents' house. They went about their benign routines with the four of us kids underfoot for two whole months.

Sundays, Papa preached at Woodland Shores and we returned from church at noon to the aroma of Grammy's pot roast in the oven. After the meal and cleanup, Grammy sat in her velour swivel chair and worked on a crossword puzzle. Papa watched whatever baseball game happened to be on, and then he always fell asleep in his La-Z-Boy recliner. When he awoke around 3:30, he asked Grammy if there happened to be any ice cream on hand. Of course there was. And one of us grandchildren went scrambling to grab the gallon of vanilla from the giant freezer in the garage. (The one who helped fetch it got to have some first.)

Grammy clipped her beloved rose bushes after dinner. On Tuesdays Papa went to the church to begin work on another week's sermon. Grammy grocery-shopped that day. On Fridays I got to help fold church bulletins and stack them neatly inside shoe boxes for Sunday morning. My grandparents' lives possessed a rhythm, a routine, as soothing to me as waves on the beach. I gravitated to the rhythm and curled up inside it like a tiny animal that lives inside a shell. I never wanted to leave Bridgman.

I had trouble sleeping as a child, but not in Bridgman. My bedroom at Grammy and Papa's was affectionately called the sewing room, because it housed all of Grammy's sewing and quilting materials. In it was a twin bed that had once been my uncle Allyn's. At night I lay in the sewing room twin bed with a view of the open closet where Grammy kept quilts in progress. From there I overheard my conservative, gentle grandparents whispering to each other about the day, about things to come for tomorrow, and about small details that floated to the surface before sleep overtook them.

What people wanted to ask me about growing up in the way I did was, *Can you tell me what it means to have a home?* They wanted to ask me, but they didn't have the language for it, and I was only a child. They thought, *How would she know? She's just a young girl.*

Instead, people asked me a standard set of questions: How many places have you lived? Which was your favorite place? Which was the worst place to live? But what they really wanted to know were other things. When I said I didn't really have a home, they shivered for themselves... displacement at the core of every heart. People have a haunting need to know a place is theirs forever, and a deep fear that it isn't.

Because I didn't have a permanent home, I wrestled better and harder than most adults with the need for one. By the time I was a teenager I had burned through to finally create an expanded definition of *home*.

I began to sense that maybe home had less to do with staying in one place and more to do with returning somewhere and to someone. I was catching a glimpse of the whole.

From my twin bed in the sewing room, I could see Grammy's quilts taking shape, where she hung them in the closet. I noticed that she often used one color as a base and then placed patterned pieces, sometimes very different patterns, in between the colored base squares. When done like that, the patterned pieces didn't seem so incongruous. As long as they had the colored buffer square next to them, the styles of the other squares could be as different as you wanted. The colored blocks were the consistency the quilt needed.

Bridgman was my color block squares—a bright yellow two months—in between the city we left and the city to which we were headed. As long as I returned to Bridgman every summer, the years of traveling, like crazy, patterned squares, could be endured.

CHAPTER 9

FITTING IN

Throughout our moves, my siblings and I sometimes met kids like us who had moved around a lot. We'd compare lists of cities and our fathers' jobs. These kids who had moved around—sometimes as often as I had—understood the unwritten means for getting by as the new kid. There were ways to survive the social complexities of it. And by the time I was in sixth grade, living in Montreal, Quebec, in Canada, I could tell you without hesitation that surviving as the new kid in town meant blending in.

On my first day of school in Montreal, my brother Eric and I got a crash course in Canadian pride from a playground bully. Foolishly, we had assumed that Canadians were just like our family unit: not particularly loyal to any one country or political ideology, mostly westernized in consumer tastes and beliefs, and comfortable being called North Americans. We were dead wrong.

"Eh! Eh, you Americans!?" It was not so much a question as a scowled accusation. Apparently we weren't meant to answer with a proud, "You bet!" Truth was, we didn't really know what to say. It was, after all, kind of a trick question for us Marshall kids. It was the cousin question to the dreaded, "Where are you from?" Our silence seemed to fuel the boy's hostility. "You Americans think you know everything. You think everything good comes from America. Well, it doesn't! Where were your bikes made?"

Eric and I exchanged blank looks. Where were our bikes made? Did it matter? I could only picture the pastel *Huffy* painted on the middle bar of my bike, which was propped up by the back door of our house, barely a week out of the moving van. Where were Huffys made? I sensed enough not to say, "Made in the good ol' US of A, thank you very much." Eric and I shrugged.

"Well, good bikes are made in Canada too, you know!" Finally, an opportunity to agree. We nodded largely; surely some great bicycles are made in Canada.

Then the boy pointed in our faces. "What do you know about hockey?" We didn't imagine that we'd have to know enough for a quiz on the first day of school. We hadn't foreseen the all-encompassing pride these people took in their hockey teams. Then, suddenly, the patriotic bully gave us the best advice a new kid could hope for:

"If you live here," he said, pointing his finger at the pebbly playground, a speck of earth on the vast Canadian landscape, "you need to know all about the Montreal Canadiens. They are the best, better than any American hockey team." With that last flare of nationalism, he turned in a whirl and left us.

We were like ponies hearing the feed bag shake. We went cantering home that day, famished to learn from newspapers, books and TV everything we could cram into our little brains about the Montreal Canadiens. That year, hockey would be our means for fitting in.

We became megafans, obsessed—the kind of fans who paint their faces with the Canadiens' *C* in blue, white, and red. We became chest-slapping, loud, obnoxious fans. To really know the Montreal people, and to embrace our lives that year, our family needed to catch the fan fever for the Montrealers' national team. The people of Montreal had been scheduling their lives—vacations and weddings—around season games. Moreover, hockey itself was imbedded into the consciousness of the Canandian people and was part of the country's master calendar of events, woven into their conception of the seasons.

Never before that year in Montreal had my family gathered around a sports game with such intensity. Until then, I had never heard my dad cheer for a particular team. He played tame sports, like golf. He didn't talk about sports with any masculine growl. But that year in Montreal, I saw him yell and wave his fists with the most devoted hockey fans. We watched him, and we watched each other, fall in love with hockey. We caught the fever, and it was grand.

Every Saturday evening, long after darkness had defeated daylight over those right-angled provinces, families all over Canada crowded around their television sets to watch Hockey Night in Canada. We cheered and moaned wins and losses by turns, and then we crawled to our beds reluctantly, sorry to face life outside the sound of slapping sticks and skates. At Dad's office, as at our school on Monday, we discussed with passion the details of the game. No one could bear to wait another week for the next game. Finally, we seemed to fit in.

What better "in" with our new hockey know-it-all friends than to literally *know* (or have our dad know) someone who played for the Montreal Canadiens. Ryan Walter, number 11, was known for his Christian faith. He was chosen as the chairman of the men's committee for the Montreal BGEA crusade. He was a kind man, somewhat quiet for a rough hockey player.

Dad's position on the organizing committee meant that he frequently sat at meetings with Ryan Walter, the two even exchanging tidbits about their families. In my imagination, this meant that Ryan Walter was a big fan of Jess Marshall. The thought of it was more lovely than a freshly Zambonied rink.

Eric got to take advantage of the association with Ryan Walter. He invited his friend Rob to come down to the rink one Saturday afternoon to watch the team practice. Eric and Rob could hardly stand their excitement or keep their butts in their stadium seats, which was good because at one point Walter called out to Eric, "Hey, Marshall! Catch these!" And for about ten glorious minutes,

Ryan Walter flicked pucks out into the stands for Eric and Rob to scramble after.

Heather pulled away from the family unit that year in Montreal. She was a high school freshman and had always been quieter than me, so it wasn't strange when she declined to play a game of Uno or to watch a movie with us. But Mom noticed a difference in Heather's behavior—the way mothers do.

At night in bed, Mom ran her hands along the edging of her own mother's quilt, absently feeling for the detailed stitching, for the pattern. Her instincts told her that there was a reason for her oldest daughter's distant behavior and that it had to do with an intense need to fit in.

I could imagine Heather choking on the reason for our move to Montreal as she stood in an apathetic group of ninth grade peers. "Our dad is here in, um, Montreal to help Mr. Graham, um, preach ..." The rest, the real name of God, was left unspoken because it was often socially isolating.

Sometimes after school, Heather brought home her wild friend, Christina Rausch. Christina's dad and mom were divorced, and neither of them showed much interest in their daughter's life. Her dad was the announcer for the Canadiens' hockey games at the Forum.

Christina dyed her hair as black as a crow and used eyeliner like paint around her eyes, which glittered like a bird's when she and Heather whispered in the kitchen while raiding the pantry for junk food. I hung around the corner, watching them. I was afraid of Christina. She rolled her eyes openly, brazenly, at nearly every comment Mom or Dad made. At the dinner table, we prayed over our food. All eyes were closed, expect mine and Christina's. I watched her watch Heather. She pierced a look at Heather. *Forget this Christian stuff.* I worried for my sister.

Christina had no one waiting up for her at home, but Heather did. And Heather knew exactly what she could expect when she lurked home after sneaking out at night. That year there were lots of quiet talks with Heather behind Mom and Dad's closed doors. When it came time to move again, this time to Glasgow, Scotland, Mom was relieved to uproot her brood.

We all worked hard at fitting in, but sometimes fitting in was nearly impossible. I was thirteen when we moved to Glasgow, our tenth move with Billy Graham. It was, without contest, the most difficult year of my childhood.

Various elements were stacked against me that year in Scotland, ones that I could not control. All year long in Glasgow, I tried in vain to carve a space for myself. I tried to create a sense of belonging in Scotland, however temporal, but it never took.

The first time I set foot in our rented row home on Marlborough Avenue, I knew it was to be a doomed year. The house was an old Victorian row home owned and furnished by Communist Hungarians. This was strange, even by our loose renters' standards. We had lived in some wilting houses, ones that needed repairs or paint touch-ups or that perpetually smelled like wet dog. But never had we lived in a house filled with someone else's furniture, clandestine books, and artwork.

To make matters more strange, my bedroom was eight feet long and six feet wide. You had to step down and practically turn sideways to enter it. The bed was built into the wall because it was the only way to fit one in the room. The room was the precise size and had the exact feel of a dingy ship's cabin. I was being squeezed out. The house said, *You don't belong here.* I heard it loud and clear.

Heather, Allison, and I attended the prestigious Westbourne School for Girls in Glasgow, established in 1877. The school met in an enormous old Victorian manor, seated high up on Great Western Road. Much to my horror, the school uniform looked like something an elderly SWAT team member might wear, a lot of shifty polyester and thick wool. And it was entirely purple.

On my first day of school at Westbourne, a dowdy secretary led me through the maze of hallways to find my first class. This gave me a chance to inspect the strange mansion they called a school. *I will never find my way out of this building,* I thought to myself. And I was right. For the next eight months, I stumbled around that wintry manor like Jane Eyre at Thornfield.

The secretary led me through narrow hallways whose baseboards creaked. I then followed her up winding staircases. We passed classrooms that were once bedchambers, each one with a yawning old fireplace. The girls inside shot me quizzical looks as I walked by the rooms, and then turned back to their books and "jotters."

"Ms. Brooks, this is a new student. She is from America," said the secretary. The Scottish accent turned the statement into a sort of rhetorical question.

"Oh my, then have a seat right here. We'll get you a syllabus and supplies list right short. The change bell will ring soon."

At least two of Ms. Brooks' phrases I didn't catch—something about my being short or needing to change into shorts? Then an obnoxious buzzer vibrated the wall. Chairs scraped the old wood floors as girls got up to leave. I followed, with not a single inclination where I was headed. No one had informed me of my schedule.

The rest of that first day was a blur.

The Scottish accent was baffling. I had lived in France, where the French language flirted with you like a satin ribbon, but Scotland's English tangled me up like a thick jump rope. On that first day of school, I understood only two or three words out of every sentence spoken.

At lunch, the girls only seemed curious about my being American, not genuinely interested in being friends. One freckled girl leaned into my face with "prawn-crisp" breath and honestly wanted to know if I knew Michael Jackson. Was I from Hollywood or New York City?

She was in earnest, and waiting for my reply.

I wanted to fit in. "Well, I've been to Disney World." I might have omitted that I had been two years old at the time of that trip.

"What do you wear in American schools?" Now that was a decent question, an appropriate question.

"Oh, we just wear pants," I answered.

The whole table erupted in laughter, the kind of showy laughter that wants to draw attention from other parts of the room.

"Pants! You just wear pants?" They clamored at once.

I sat there in my purple skirt and saggy tights. What was wrong with pants? I wished I were in pants. I'd have given my right arm to be in a pair of pants.

"I mean, you know, like jeans or whatever," I said, my face a beating red heart.

"Oh," one girl said, hushing the others, "you mean *trousers*."

Papa and Grammy Decker were the only people on the planet I knew who used the word *trousers*. It was a word like *davenport*, completely ridiculous, the kind of outdated word that sent my cousins and me into fits of mocking laughter. And now here were girls my age with pimples and neon scrunchies using *trousers* like it was normal. It was suddenly like Opposite Day on *You Can't Do That on Television*. *Trousers* was a cool word in Scotland. I was exhausted from trying to fit in.

"Pants are what you wear, you know, underneath … *here*," said a quieter girl, pointing at her skirt.

"Oh, you mean underwear," I clarified again, my head hurting.

But then the change bell rang and lunch was over. I desperately hoped the girls would understand that I wasn't a complete loser and that I didn't only wear Fruit of the Looms to school in America.

The quiet girl who had spoken up walked with me to our next class. Through the heavy accent, I gathered that her name was Claire, that she lived somewhere near my house, and that she had a little sister named Anna. I had to narrow all my attention on her mouth as she spoke just to catch that much. The rest was alphabet soup.

About a month into my Scottish school year, the track-suited PE teacher approached me after gym class one day. (I was just changing out of the purple pampers they called a gym uniform.)

"So, I hear you play hockey."

"Well, not really. I mean I played street hockey sometimes last year in Canada," I confessed.

"Right, then! Show up at our hockey field on Saturday and we'll add you to the team," she turned in a whirl.

It was the first time anyone wanted to include the "cheeky American gul" in anything at Westbourne. I went home and proudly reported the news.

That Saturday morning, Dad drove me to the school hockey field. My stomach did a nervous backflip when I saw the girls on the field all wearing short skirts and knee socks (all purple, of course), and whacking what looked to be croquet balls down the field. Somehow I had convinced myself that field hockey would be like ice hockey, just without the ice.

The coach saw me, waved me over, and issued me a skirt and knee socks. "I suppose your trainers will have to do, since you don't seem to have cleats." Did she say something about me not having a personal trainer?

"Stand over here, Marshall. When I give you the signal, you'll take Catrina's place."

I wasn't entirely sure which girl was Catrina. The next series of minutes was a blur. I had planned on watching the game, to get a feel for the sport. But I got distracted by a wheeling seagull. It dove and soared and cawed, reminding me very much of my sweet summer days on Lake Michigan. I closed my eyes and could almost imagine the waves crashing down on the shore.

"Marshall, you're in!" The coach literally pushed me forward, over the field boundary line. Then someone smacked the ball in my direction. It stopped at my feet. I stood there for a moment holding my cane (or hockey stick, as they called it). I could hear girls yelling, "Shoot, shoot!" I looked and saw the goalie and a net. So I did what they told me to do: I shot the ball with the stick as hard as I could. It went right past the bewildered goalie, right into my own team's net.

After that everything got very quiet. No more seagull. No more happy girls playing hockey. The only sound was of an angry

Scottish dad on the sideline, pointing at me, yelling, "Get her off the fieeeeeld!"

I was never asked to play for the field hockey team again.

By April of my year in Scotland, I had stopped trying to fit in. Every time I opened my mouth at school, it was obvious that I was a foreigner. I thought I was handling the sense of isolation pretty well, but one day a girl from an upper grade cornered me at lunch and called me "a daft American."

Something like hot tar boiled up inside me and spilled over the edges. I hauled back and punched her square in the nose. It felt great. But I was an impish thirteen-year-old girl, so the punch didn't do any damage or shut her up. It only incited her anger.

"Go back to America!" she screamed as she held her reddened nose.

"I wish I could!" was all I could manage to say, the tears pouring down my face, blurring everyone in a true purple haze. She ran to tell the prefect that the daft American was also "a violent beasty."

When people have hard days at work, they retreat home to lick their wounds and to be held by the furniture that knows their shape. The paintings and baubles on the walls reflect back to them their happier times. But the Hungarian Communists' house was not ours. Not one stick of furniture or picture on the wall could whisper back to me a sense of peace.

When I could not get warm or comfortable in my ship's cabin bed at night, I got up in the pitch-dark. But I had nowhere to go that was mine. I wandered to the living room couch, but it did not sigh when I lay down on it. I had no imprint on that couch.

No object in that Scottish house held my shape after I had left. No carpet in any room was worn because of my feet. In the Scotland nights, I had nowhere to go that was mine. I had never felt less at home. Where did I belong?

CHAPTER 10

CERTAIN OF WHAT SHE COULD NOT SEE

No other city challenged Mom's eye handicap more than Glasgow, Scotland. Because the school system in Glasgow did not provide buses, Mom had to drive us kids to school every day. At that point in her life it was still legal for her to drive, though with great caution and, as Dad liked to say, "with her pit crew of angels around the car."

After my first day of school in Glasgow, I ran out to our car, a blue compact station wagon we were renting that year. Mom waved at me from what looked like the passenger side of the car. It was still strange to see people driving on the other side of the road. I ran to get the shotgun seat before my sisters could.

"Hi, honey. How was your day?" Mom's tone was all wrong, and she was sniffling. I looked at her face. It was red and blotchy. Her eyes were puffy. She had been crying. This was upsetting after an already very unsettling first day.

"Why are you crying, Mom?" The question sounded more demanding than I'd intended.

"Oh, I'm just having a hard time ... adjusting." With that, she erupted in a fresh wave of tears.

Heather and Allison were in the car by then, listening. No verbal explanation ensued, but in a second we understood. Our mother's frustrations became suddenly obvious when she tried to pull out into traffic.

"Mom, look out for that car!" I screamed.

"Oh my goodness … I don't know how to do this! Lord Jesus, help me!" Mom blubbered even as she yanked and pummeled the shift knob.

"Mom, do you know how to drive a stick shift?" Heather dared to ask what we all were wondering.

"Well …" She still hadn't actually pulled out into the left lane or answered the question. Her eyes darted from the rearview mirror on her left to the shift knob and then to the street. Over and over again she checked these vitals. It seemed we would never leave the school parking zone.

Allison, nine, had had her own exhausting first day, like all of us, and decided that Mom's present driving predicament wasn't worth losing sleep over. She popped two favorite fingers into her mouth, leaned back, and eased into a nap, not the least bit bothered by the yelling, crying, and honking.

"Okay, Mom, go now. Now!" Heather yelled.

"Oh Lord, here we go! Hang on!" Mom wailed.

We were out, that is, out in the middle of traffic on Kelvinside Road, but then the car stalled out.

"Mom, what are you doing?!" I was, hands down, the least helpful child in our family.

"I'm trying, Jess. Do not yell at me!" Mom turned the key, and the car hummed back to life. She took another deep breath, stepped on a pedal I had never seen in a car, and rammed the gearshift in the direction of my right thigh. The car lurched forward.

It seemed we were going to be okay; the car was moving along like the other cars on the road. But then we came to a stoplight—on an incline.

"Oh no, hang on, girls!" Once the light turned green, the wrong thing happened. We slipped backward like a slug, heading straight for the front bumper of the car behind us.

He was probably a very nice Scotsman, regular and congenial enough in his ordinary Glaswegian life, but in that moment, the man in the car behind us turned William Wallace.

He leaned out his window, his shaggy beard in the wind. "What are you doooing, you daft eegit! Away an bile yer heid!"

"What's he saying?" we all screamed.

"Lord, you alone can help me now." I had never heard Mom pray like that before. She was both slain in the Spirit and ready to punch someone. We were slipping downward, fast.

Mom thrust all her energy into her left foot, let up on the brake and stepped on the gas pedal with the faith of a saint. We lurched forward just in time. Cursing William Wallace had been halfway out his window. We made it up and over the hill. Eric's school, Kelvinside Academy, was down at the bottom, and we were already twenty-five minutes late to pick up our brother after his first day of school.

Mom did her best to round the bend at the bottom of the hill, grinding the gears. Eric turned his head at the noise. I thought I saw him cringe.

With a jolt, we stopped right in front of him. In a flash, he jumped in next to Heather, who eased Allison's purple figure, amazingly still asleep, over to the other side of the seat.

"Hi, honey. How was your first day?" Mom tried to sound welcoming, like the place to be was our death-trap of a car.

"I hate it here." My brother was usually phlegmatic, so this emotional eruption was very unlike him, even on a first day of school. "These Scottish people are the weirdest!"

I nodded my ascent.

"What happened?" Mom tried to sound surprised, as if her own day had been such cake.

"I tried talking to the guys in my class, but they use the strangest words!"

It was my own assessment exactly. I loved my brother very much in that moment.

"I didn't understand anything they said all day. Then, I was standing here waiting for you to pick me up with these two guys standing next to me. I overheard them talking."

"And …?" Mom had turned her body to face Eric, who was in the backseat. She listened like the good mom she was.

"The one boy turned to his friend standing under an umbrella and said, 'Waiting for Mummy, dear?' And the umbrella kid smiled all stupid and answered, 'Aye, and keeping dry!'" Eric searched our faces for empathy. "It was the gayest thing I'd ever heard!"

Normally our mother would chasten us heartily for using the word *gay*. Christian families didn't acknowledge that word, let alone that lifestyle. But this time she said nothing. Instead, her face began to change into a smile, and then the merest little laugh slipped out. Before we knew it, she was cracking up. Seeing our mother lose it like that was incredible. It was catching. We all began laughing, and then our laughter turned to hilarity—the kind of sidesplitting howls that make you cry. You slip over into tears, but you don't care anymore.

Everything spilled out. We couldn't breathe in the best kind of way.

"Waiting for Mummy, dear? … Aye, and keeping dry!" We all repeated it. Over and over again we said it for each other and then laughed ourselves stupid over such phrasing. We must have sat there cracking ourselves up for ten minutes, steaming up our rented wagon with stress-releasing laughter.

Finally, Mom pulled out of Kelvinside's parking zone, this time with only a few grinding jolts—and none of us even cared.

Mom called those years an adventure because something in her wanted that kind of life. But the Spirit in her called them sanctification. Sometimes the life we want and the life God wants for us can dovetail so precisely, so beautifully, that it leaves us speechless with laughter and a sense of grace—laughter from my lovely mother, who had never seen the stars but who, by faith, was certain of what she could not see.

CHAPTER 11

THE LOCKED ROOM

In Scotland, the Communist Hungarians rented us their house for one year, and all but one bedroom were we permitted to enter. Before our arrival, they had collected all their most precious belongings, piled them into a bedroom, and then locked that bedroom's door.

For all I knew, the key to that door was far away in the father's breast pocket somewhere deep inside Eastern Europe. Every nerve ending in my body tingled when I passed by that locked room. My overly sensitive nature was completely undone by the enigma of it.

I did not trust the people who had locked the door, so how could I trust what they'd stored inside it? I feared the mysterious contents behind the door. I feared being locked in. And yet, truth be told, I feared that the secret to my peace of mind was somehow veiled by that door.

The house itself was built in the early 1900s, and the original doors, which all bore the old warded-lock keyholes, were still intact. These keyholes were the kind that children instinctively want to peer through.

Only I wasn't brave enough to put my eye to the keyhole on the locked door. I wanted to, but I was petrified of what horror might be staring back at me. I picked up speed whenever I passed by the room, which was fairly often since I had to pass it to get to my parents' bedroom. The door seemed to hum like radioactive matter.

It buzzed and swelled in my ears, the same swelling sound I heard before a panic attack.

By February of our year in Scotland, I was suppressing panic attacks nearly every day. My brain felt as though it were spinning like a top toward the very edge of sanity, toward a total meltdown. I was only thirteen, but I wrestled with big questions like an adult.

I feared death and the incalculable, ever-expanding size of the universe. I feared the term *forever* because I couldn't fathom the concept. I feared and dreaded that heaven would be a place I did not recognize, that it would be like another house in an unfamiliar neighborhood. Worse, it would be the house where I was living, with a thousand locked rooms and interminable mystery behind every door.

In an effort to tamp my panic concerning deep, philosophical topics, I sought distraction. I had heard somewhere that cigarettes helped calm people down. I needed calming. I needed something to hold, something bad but not evil, and I knew there was a difference.

"Let's buy cigarettes," I whispered to my neighbor friend, Claire one evening in the early spring.

"Wha? We're not sixteen! You are crazy, Jess." I loved the way her Scottish accent made my name sound.

"Why not? Have you ever smoked?"

"Nooo. Have yuuuu?"

I had to be honest. "Well, no, not really." In Montreal my brother went through a particular pyrotechnic phase, using a magnifying glass as a lighter. We'd found an old cigarette butt near the gutter and relit it, but neither of us had had the courage to put it to our lips.

"Let's go to the newsagent's stand and get a pack."

Claire laughed her hearty guffaw, but I could tell she would oblige.

"Your dad smokes a pipe; go get his matches." I could boss Claire around like that. She had a naturally buoyant spirit that didn't take things personally. I would really miss Claire when I left Scotland.

Off she ran through her scruffy backyard while I waited in the sunset half-light, feeling alive and focused for the first time that year.

Claire returned giggling with the matches in her fist. I stuffed them into my jacket pocket and pulled at her arm to follow me. We made a plan as we ran.

"We should go to the newsagent on Crow Road. It's farther from our houses—less chance that someone will recognize us."

"Okay! This is daft!" Claire huffed and squealed.

I skipped a beat in my step. Running felt good in my knees. We arrived at the corner of busy Crow Road before I'd had time to think up our next move. We stopped abruptly, laughing and coughing in the cool air.

"Now what?" Claire giggled. "I'm too scared to buy them!"

I stared hard at the newsagent store. "I'll do it."

Would the Indian man even sell them to me? I saw Scottish girls and boys my age smoking outside the discos. Where did they get their fags, as cigarettes were called in Scotland? I would have to take my chances.

"How much do they cost?" I asked.

"Ha! I dinnieken!" Claire's funny Scottish vernacular bubbled up in her nervousness.

"Okay, I'll take £10." In fact, that amount of money was all I had. It was my two weeks' allowance for cleaning bathrooms.

I certainly didn't look sixteen.

The store was suddenly imposing; the old, grimy flyers that clung to its exterior flapped and swirled. They seemed to wave me away in warning, but I kept approaching. I wanted those cigarettes.

I opened the door, which clinked and beeped noisily, announcing me, *a minor*. I went right up to the counter, too nervous for browsing. The same Indian man who had sold me onion crisps last week was there again. Barely looking at me, he glared over my head at the young man rooting around in the cooler.

With my money in my left fist, I blurted out my request: "I want a pack of fags."

Then the newsagent saw me, and looked right into my sassy American mouth. "What kind?" was all he said.

It was the one thing I should have thought of ahead of time. What kind of cigarette did I want to smoke? He was going to sell them to me. All I needed to do was tell the man what kind I would like to buy. My brain felt like a Tilt-A-Whirl. I forced myself to look past him and at the shelves of cigarettes. *Think, Jess.* Then I saw it: the name of my street in Scotland. There it was, bright red and beckoning. I said the word as I had heard Scots say it over and over again. I swirled the *r*'s around in my mouth and felt for a fleeting moment like I belonged there. "Marlboros … thanks."

"Menthols or reds?"

This time I simply repeated him. "Reds," I said definitively.

I gave the man my allowance, and he handed me my first pack of cigarettes.

I rushed to the door and stumbled blindly, triumphantly, to Claire at the corner. The pack felt like a gun in my hand. I threw it to Claire, who screamed as she caught it. We ran instinctively toward an alley.

"Here, you take 'em!" Claire laughed and threw the pack back at me. I felt the cellophane wrapping and the weight of the box. It was heavier than I'd imagined and just as dangerous as I'd hoped. My cold hands ripped off the top. I threw the silver foil down at my feet. There under the lid stood three slender rows of white cigarettes. They were prettier than I'd expected. I thought of my sister Heather, of how straight and dangerously pretty she always looked. I pulled out a cigarette and held it up, ready to burn it.

"Ah cannae git the matches tae light!" Claire yelped.

I sighed, took the matches, and gave Claire the cigarette instead. After several attempts, we got the thing lit. I took the first puff and coughed, of course but lied to Claire, "It's good."

She took the hissing fag from my fingertips, and inhaled tentatively.

We walked together down the rest of the alleyway, passing that one cigarette between us, barely inhaling, but stretching our fore and middle fingers into the gesture like movie stars. I felt the buzz from the nicotine.

I lifted my eyes up to the concrete walls that never got any sunlight because in this country there wasn't any. I blew out smoke as casually and elegantly as I could. The smoke almost looked like swirling light—almost, but not quite.

The next day I experienced the worst panic attack of my young life.

I was in English class. The teacher was droning on about past participles and verb tenses. I let my mind wander, which for me was dangerous. I should have known better.

I began envisioning the blackness of outer space. In my mind's eye I saw the solitude of our planet with its infinitesimal life that would all eventually die. The certainty of this outcome shattered me. I glanced around the room—just ordinary girls lost in ordinary daydreams about boys and school. *What is wrong with me?* My hands began to sweat, and suddenly I couldn't breathe. A panic attack was coming on, and I couldn't stop it. I shot back from my chair and fled the room. I didn't know where to go. I wished someone would hit me over the head and knock me out of my misery.

After running down the narrow hallway, I rushed down a flight of stairs to the main office. By the time I pulled open the doors to the office, my brow was covered in sweat.

"I need help," was all I could manage. A secretary stood up from her chair, a look of real alarm on her face.

"Oh my, you are shaking. You look ill. We'll call home. Sit right here." She helped me down into a chair.

I was ill. In the core of my heart I was sick with fear and despair. The secretary called my house, but no one picked up.

That's because Mom and Dad have left me, I thought. All my worst fears were coming true.

"How about we find you a spot to lie down?" The woman was talking to me, but she sounded a million miles away.

I followed her lead; I had no willpower to argue. She led me up three flights of stairs to a room in that old Victorian manor that I was certain no student had ever entered. From a giant ring, she pulled out a long, rusty warded key exactly like the one that must open the locked room in our house.

With it, she unlocked the door before us and led me in. For just a moment, I was pulled to reality. Every surface of the room was painted in lapis blue, from the walls to the radiator to the ceiling. The color was vivid, and the high-gloss finish made the whole place seem to sparkle. Strangely, in the very center of the blue room was a single bed.

The woman said nothing. She just indicated with her hand that I should lie down on that bed. I sat down on it and tilted back my head to get a view of the twenty-foot-high painted ceiling. I didn't see the woman leave the room, but in the next moment I knew she was gone.

The door clicked shut.

I will never be entirely sure, but I think I heard the sound of a lock turn. It seemed she had bolted me in.

If I had feared complete and utter isolation in the universe before, if I had feared the locked room in our Hungarian Communists' house, then at that moment all my fears had come to pass. All was silence on the other side of the door. I was completely alone. Everyone, including the secretary at my school, was in on a plan to cast me off. They had all devised a scheme to lock me in a room and then head for the home I longed to find.

I was the brunt of a cosmic joke.

All I could do was lie down in defeat upon the bed. My eyes spilled over with tears of anguish.

I had never felt more helpless in my life.

And then, quite suddenly, the thought struck me that I should pray.

I opened my mouth, wet with tears and said, "Jesus." The blue room bounced the name across the surface of the walls so that I heard it said right back to me.

It sounded good, so I said it some more.

Then I told him how scared I felt. And as I talked, I realized that I was addressing someone. I was making conversation. I talked; He listened.

And it dawned on me, lying on that single bed in a lapis blue room, that if He were listening, then He was right there with me. Upon this discovery came a peace that can only be described as the best things I had known in my life up to that point.

The peace of Jesus's presence in the locked room was that of my grandparents' house in Michigan. It was that of the waves at Weko Beach, and of my father's favorite music, the Beatles and Bob Dylan, to which I listened mile after mile on road trips. It was the hint of wind chimes up ahead that I'd heard in the Bible verse Billy Graham had given me. It was the peace of a grand design for good in my life.

It was Jesus inside the room waiting for me, and never had the door been locked.

CHAPTER 12

IN MY LIFE

One dreary evening in April, I sat on the small floor space of my bedroom at our rented house on Marlborough Avenue. I held the cassette tape for *Rubber Soul*. I wanted to hear one song in particular, "In My Life." I knew the song would put to melody my new, overwhelming affection for the God that had met me at my worst moment in the locked blue room.

"Though I know I'll never lose affection for people and things that went before, in my life I've loved you more." The Beatles sang about secret lovers, and I sang along about Jesus. I was beginning to sense that this God who spoke with me in the blue room could rise like a sail on the water, outshining all others in my life. The encounter could become a relationship, if I wanted it to.

By May it was obvious that I was going to fail nearly every class at Westbourne School for Girls. Academically for me, the year was a flop, but spiritually the year would ripple on like concentric circles after a pebble is thrown into the water.

The pebble was my encounter with Christ in the locked blue room.

That day I discovered for myself that God is hidden but not locked away; is listening when we start talking; is chatting with us when we think the whole world has left us behind. I began to develop a new sense that God was for me, a sense of his presence during every bout of anxiety. God was with me, gentle as a nurse, wiping my brow, humming a favorite Beatles melody. I suddenly wanted others to know this Christ.

On the night before the crusade week was to start, my parents sat with us children around the kitchen table of our rented home and asked, "Do you kids have any friends you want to have come to the meetings?"

"I think I'll bring Claire," I said. She was mild and sweet. She wouldn't judge me if all the songs were old hymns and the prayers rather lengthy.

"I want to bring Anna too," Allison piped up.

"In fact, Mrs. Pollock said she'd like to go." Mom tagged on cheerily.

"I might take Trisha," Heather mumbled. In actuality, Heather would probably get out of going altogether. She had a knack for avoiding all things family and church oriented. Her skill at this bordered on professional hooky.

Mom spoke up again. "Eric, I'm sure Toby and Ollie would love to join you." *Love* wasn't the word Eric was thinking of, but he nodded, always eager to keep the peace. And that settled it, the same way it got settled in most cities.

By April, we each had one or two friends whose names outranked the others. When we were asked, "Who was your best friend this year?", their names blossomed from our lips. We did not have to think about it. These were the friends we took to the crusade meetings each year. By June their names were natural, their loyalties embedded. It would be very hard to leave those names in a month.

Some years Mom made a big deal about what we wore to the crusades. Stylistically it was tricky. We were headed to hear a preacher, which suggested stuffy church clothes, but the preacher would be speaking in a football stadium, which could mean local team jerseys, jeans, and even T-shirts—and I had seen people wear just that to the crusades.

Of course, when I mentioned this fact to Mom, she sharply retorted, "Yes, but those people are not the director's daughter." Alas, I fought my best, but I usually ended up in a hand-me-down skirt from Heather.

Toby and Ollie's mom didn't get the memo that her kids were not the director's sons. Poor Toby and Ollie showed up on our front doorstep the first night of the crusade in starched white button-down shirts and ties, topped off with navy blazers. They looked like mini secret service agents.

Claire, Anna, and their mom showed up in church clothes. Claire and Anna looked nervous, like they were about to attend a funeral. I felt sorry for them. I was also sorry that I didn't know how to make them feel at ease.

When we arrived at Celtic Park, Dad met us just outside the tunnel marked for the home team's entrance. He greeted all the neighbors and then gave Mom a kiss.

"Why don't you follow me? I'll take you to some reserved seats." We followed Dad in through the concrete tunnel, around corners, and down tight hallways. As we passed doorways, Dad pointed out impressive sights. "That's where the Celtic football team meets during halftime, right through that door. And that's where Mr. Graham is waiting, right now." This was my dad in full-on director mode, shoulders back, striding at a commander's clip that forced everyone with him to do a little half skip to keep up.

Then we went outside and into the stadium's floodlights. We all squinted and reeled under the vastness of the open air dome. I looked down at my small feet and then over at Claire. Her wide eyes reflected the glare of light. I watched her attention shift rapidly from one sight to another. It was a lot to take in—thousands of tiered stadium seats filled with buzzing little bodies, and so many lights shining down from the upper lip of the stadium.

Down on the stadium floor, people were dressed like my dad, in suits with name tags and title badges, hurrying along. I knew that many of those official-looking people were volunteers from Glasgow, here to serve the Billy Graham team in any way they could. Others were my dad's team members, the men and women who, like we did, traveled from city to city to prepare for this evening and the four more after it this week.

Mom; the three of us girls; Mrs. Pollock and her girls; Eric; and Toby and Ollie sat down in a row of seats marked with reserved signs. If it had been a Celtics game, we would have had the best seats in the house, just a few rows up from the field, which was now covered by the world's biggest blanket—one huge, soft mesh blanket spreading over the entire field from end to end so as not to ruin the delicate grass.

At the far left end of the enormous field was the platform where Mr. Graham would speak. That platform was a monstrous construction, like a giant parade float. All around the perimeter of the stage were enormous fake ferns and flower arrangements. On the stage were four rows of seats reserved for the evening's special guests: political figures like city mayors and governors; Mrs. Graham; and any special musical guests.

It was church on the grandest scale—and it was my father's job to orchestrate it all.

I saw in the faces of our guests that they were impressed now, more than they were nervous about being in church. It was hard to be nervous anymore. You found yourself to be one of thousands of people at an event that was suddenly bigger, more significant, than your personal baggage about church.

Old George Beverly Shea sang "I'd Rather Have Jesus." I could tell that Claire and Anna were bored by it. I didn't blame them. What was to like about an old man belting out a crusty hymn? Not much, but for me his voice was a comforting old quilt. I'd been hearing him sing that song all my life. My affection for him stemmed all the way back to that evening at our house in Alaska when he graciously ate the ruined dinner biscuits I'd made.

After he sat down to much applause, Sir David McNee, chairman of Mission Scotland, commissioner to the Metropolitan

Police in London, went to the podium. Then the whole stadium erupted in genuinely loving applause. He was a familiar face, and his appearance made everyone feel at home. He spoke more passionately than they had ever heard before. He talked briefly but intensely about God's love for us all. And then he turned to indicate Mr. Graham, who was walking up on stage.

There was movement in the high rafter seats and in the seats around me. People were standing up to applaud. Down below, camera people from news stations around the country skittered around like black ants to get a good shot. We all got up and clapped. Sir David McNee shook Billy Graham's hand warmly and then bowed out. The clapping for Mr. Graham continued for a full two minutes.

It's always this way, I thought to myself. I stopped clapping and just watched. I never got tired of it. I liked to imagine that the thousands and thousands of strangers there that night were applauding my father's job and for my life inside of that job. I was overwhelmed with gratitude.

Mr. Graham only raised his hand before the sound of clapping diminished to something more like gentle rain, "Thank you, thank you. Please, please have a seat."

First Mr. Graham opened his Bible and told the audience what Scripture he would read that night. Then he read from his big, thick Bible and began his message. I found myself holding my breath. My hands were clenched on the edges of my plastic stadium seat. I'd heard this man speak every year for as long as I could remember. It was echoes of his voice I heard when I read my Bible. It was nearly impossible for me to imagine that the thousands of people there could feel anything less than complete admiration for him.

After his message, Mr. Graham lifted his head and looked up at the rafter seats—and then he talked right to people's hearts. He told them about God's love. He didn't use emotional language. He said things in a declarative, affirmative way that left people silent.

He said, "You are probably alone and scared. You wonder what the purpose of life is, and you have no answers."

He didn't criticize them for it; he didn't denounce their questions.

Then Mr. Graham did what seemed impossible with thousands and thousands of people in the crowd. He told people to get up out of their seats. He told us that it was time. He said, "It's time to get up out of your seat and stand in front of this podium, and to say by coming forward, I want to follow Jesus Christ. I need Him in my life. You won't be alone, as others will come too. It will take four or five minutes if you are coming down from the top"—he said this last while pointing at the shadowed people in the highest bleacher seats—"but I will wait."

Claire leaned over to me and whispered, "I want to go forward and invite Jesus into my heart." Her eyes were full of tears. They reflected back to me the tears I had shed that day in the locked blue room. My heart filled with hope for my friend. I was ready to walk down to the field and stand with her.

Claire turned to her mom to ask if she could do that. I didn't hear the conversation, but I saw Mrs. Pollock shake her head no. It was an embarrassed no. Mrs. Pollock's face stayed red the entire rest of the night. Usually very chatty, she was silent and formal on the way home that night.

Nothing would have made me happier than to walk Claire forward into that decision at a Billy Graham crusade, and I realized this all at once as I lay in my ship cabin bed later that night. It struck me with perfect clarity that it was for such a moment that Billy Graham prayed on stage with his head bowed.

I saw myself in years to come, still wishing I had had the chance to walk Claire forward into a relationship with Christ at an event my father had so beautifully orchestrated. My disappointment spilled over into waves of tears.

CHAPTER 13

BACK IN THE USA

I thought that returning to the United States would give me back a sense of belonging that had been absent my year in Scotland. After all, my passport declared me an American citizen. I had assumed that by sloughing off that itchy, purple Scottish school uniform, I could slide right back into American life, like a well-worn pair of Levi's jeans. But, as I discovered, you can't go backwards.

We flew back to the United States during the late summer of 1991. Papa Decker retrieved our vitamin-D-deficient bodies from the Chicago airport and stopped to let me out at the edge of Donna Drive so that I could run the length of it, straight into my grandmother's arms, outside their faithful home.

Grammy spread beach blankets down for us at Weko Beach. We didn't object. We lay there like washed-up lake debris for a whole summer. Then, Dad told us one night around Grammy's kitchen table that we'd be moving to Philadelphia, Pennsylvania, and the feeling of being utterly foreign overtook me anew. *Here we go again,* I said to myself. *Another home that will never feel like home.*

When it came to starting at another school again, I took comfort in thinking that I was not a foreigner in the strict sense anymore. I had survived fistfights in Scotland over my national identity. I had weathered countless stares and unsavory comments over my flat accent. I was an American in America now; how hard could it be to fit in to a typical American junior high?

On my first day of school in Philadelphia, I found my way through the chatty halls of Paxon Hollow Middle School to English class.

The teacher called roll. I heard the boy sitting in front of me say that his name was PJ Kennedy. The teacher then arrived at me. "Marshall?" she asked.

"Yes, Jessica Marshall." That was all I said, but PJ Kennedy whipped around in his seat like a tetherball. "You talk weird," he announced for the class.

I kept my mouth closed; I wasn't going to give him more material.

"Where are you from?" He spat the question in my face, the dreaded question of my life. The answer was so layered it necessitated that the asker be truly interested. I didn't sense genuine interest from PJ Kennedy. But the teacher had also paused to hear my answer.

"I just moved from Scotland," I said as quietly as I could.

"Scotland? How weird! Did you live in Scotland Yard? Why did you move here?"

I wanted to strangle this dumb kid. But thankfully the teacher had had enough and moved on with the roll.

I lowered myself as much as I could into my desk. It was like my first day in Scotland all over again. I had tried so hard to fit in there, even subduing my American accent. I had no idea that I had picked up the merest hint of a Scottish accent. It seemed I was doomed for a constant cycle of humiliation as a foreigner, no matter what my passport said.

I wasn't the only one in our family who felt a sudden sense of unfamiliarity back in the USA. Dad was trying to adjust as well. Philadelphia would be his twentieth crusade with Billy Graham. He wasn't a novice to the process and the pacing of a Billy Graham crusade. He could lead a team month by month through the necessary hoops in order to pull off the crusades, but he wasn't prepared for what he first saw in Philadelphia.

After getting settled in our home in Newtown Square, just northwest of the city, Dad arranged to meet with Dr. Bill Moore and Judge Nelson Diaz. Dr. Moore was one of Philadelphia's powerhouse African American preachers who had been chosen to represent the city churches to the BGEA. Judge Diaz was the highest-ranking judge in the Court of Common Pleas, First Judicial District of Philadelphia. The two men invited Dad to take a tour with them of America's eighth largest city.

They picked Dad up in Nelson Diaz's car and drove east into the heart of Philadelphia. Dad sat in the backseat while the two men chatted amicably up front as they drove toward North Broad Street. Moore and Diaz, on city committees together, were aware of each other's key roles in their beloved city.

But they didn't know Dad—a very white, very blond, blue-eyed, confident man who'd arrived in their city supposedly to prepare the way for a great, sweeping evangelical movement. Both men agreed that Mr. Graham was an extraordinarily gifted man of God. And in their own way, Diaz and Moore were zealous for the straightforward gospel message they knew he would preach to thousands of Philadelphians. But they needed my father to apprehend the current state of things in their city.

First they drove down into Old City—to the famous tourist spots. There was the Liberty Bell on its brick podium, the red cobbled streets, and the Georgian-styled Independence Hall. They pointed out One Liberty Place and city hall, and then they toured up the Avenue of the Arts with its theaters and fine restaurants. Diaz and Moore nodded richly. Dad remarked on the finesse and largesse of these sights, and on just how much of our country's incredible history resided there. The men smiled at Dad, his enthusiasm somewhat like that of a child's.

Then Diaz drove out of Old City and headed north up Spring Garden Street into what is known as lower north Philadelphia. Dad stopped talking, because he really didn't have any words for what he began to see: burned-out row homes, crumbling, infested crack houses, and block after block of blown-out buildings. There was graffiti everywhere—he couldn't get over the graffiti—blasted over every blank surface. Then they drove into east Philadelphia. "This is what they call the Bad Lands," Moore said. Row after row of houses looked bombed out, gaping, windowless. Everywhere people stood around street corners, their faces vacant and hurting.

Dad felt lost. "I had no idea," he mumbled.

Nelson Diaz reached out and laid his hand on Dad's knee. "This city needs help, brother." The two men knew the heartbeat of the streets and the disparity between the rich and the poor. They loved their city in all its prestigious history and culture and in its total depravity.

They were completely invested in their community.

So were the kids in our Philadelphia neighborhoods. Ethnic Italian and Greek families lived three and four generations in the same neighborhoods in our northwest suburbs. They shared a sense of pride for their turf—something I knew nothing about.

The Pennsylvania Department of Education required that students in the eighth grade learn Pennsylvania history. That was funny, since I didn't know even basic US history. My schema of facts about the country from which I hailed was like a rickety medicine man's cart, baubles of information hanging loosely to mirrors, threaded precariously around glass jars that were filled with weird stuff.

Such were the tidbits of information I had picked up somewhere and had retained, just in case. I came into town all clackety-clacking; no teacher knew what to make of my skill set. *Does she or doesn't she know how to convert fractions? What was that mnemonic device she just used?*

I knew more about the storming of the Bastille than I did about the forming of the United States government. Oddly, I could name all the natural resources in each Canadian province, and I was quite knowledgeable about the Native American tribes that hailed from upstate New York. I could label a map of Great Britain, but I didn't know a thing about America's role in any of the world wars. A scan of my brain would have revealed a giant mess.

By wintertime I had shed that hint of a Scottish accent. Dad was humbly making headway on the Philadelphia crusade, slated for June 1992.

At lunchtimes, I bought the soft, doughy pretzels that seemed a staple to the Philly diet. I was making friends, although I couldn't get used to the flinty Philly tones. Philadelphians said "I love you" the same way Heather said "Get out of my room!"

Philadelphia still did not feel like home, nor did I try to make it one. I assumed we would move again in June, so I didn't pay much attention to my geographic surroundings.

One cold November evening, my new friend, Patty, and I stayed after school late to watch the boys' basketball team practice. We giggled and flirted with the sweaty boys until her mom came to pick us up in her Pontiac Grand Prix.

"Get in, it's flippin' cold!" Patty's mom laughed and barked. She blew her cigarette smoke at us as we climbed into the backseat.

"Mouuum, you are so embarrassing!" Patty yelled. I noticed the full force of her blue-collar Philly accent, "Why do you have to smoke with the caur windouws up? You wanna kill your oown kid?"

Patty's bold sass induced a fit of laughter from Pat, but there was still no relief from the smoke. The windows didn't budge.

"Hi. Your Patty's frien.' Her only one so far, ha!" Pat switched the cig from her right hand to her left hand and then reached back to shake mine. I might have grinned, but I probably looked more shocked by the way these people talked to each other. Their tones felt like a fistfight.

"Aw-right, Jess, where do you lev?" Pat demanded. And as soon as she said it, I realized I had no idea where I "leved." *What city am I in, again?*

I could picture my street and the street that led to it, but I didn't know the names. We had lived in Newtown Square for almost four months, but coasting was what I did best. I never bothered to learn the names of streets around me because we always moved. Patty and Pat were sort of picking up on as much, scowling at me.

"Uh, I live in Newtown Square."

"Ha! Okay, Jess, where in Newtown Square do you lev? Patty, you make friends with a kid that can't even tell where she levs?"

Patty started to bite her nails, nervous for me.

Pat began to drive down Paxon Hollow Road, headed toward the general area of Newtown Square, but it was pitch-black outside. I had no visual cues to help me, just thick shadowy trees.

"Where'm I goin' Jess?" Pat was taking anxious drags of her cigarette now.

"Uh," I stammered. I had my head pressed to the cold glass window, begging the streets for clues. And then I remembered a number on the street my bus turned onto to get to school. I could see the road sign in my mind's eye. It was definitely a route number.

"A number, I think."

"Ou-K ..." Pat was gonna reach back and burn my temples with her cigarette.

"I think it's a route number or something."

"Is it Route 252, pur-chance?" Again with the flinty tones.

But 252 did sound right. "Yes, that's it!" I breathed a big sigh.

"Weeell, which way on 252, Jess?" I got the feeling it was Pat's last gracious question. It was the way she said my name. It was the curb for me if I didn't know.

I took a deep breath and gambled. "North."

And I was right. As we headed down winding 252 North, I saw my street up ahead, Wyola Drive.

I couldn't get out of that car fast enough when Pat pulled into our driveway. I'd never been so happy to see one of our rental homes. I felt a wave of affection for its bricks and mortar, for the yellow lights on in the kitchen and the living room, for my family inside. I was home, lost and then found.

I didn't know it at the time, but the people of west Philly, with their flinty tones, would become an essential part of my life for years to come. I didn't know that Philadelphia would be the last place we moved to and the first place we stayed.

In the coming years, our family would blend into the west Philadelphia suburbs like cream into coffee, until the city could not separate us from them, until we helped to make the place what it was. I didn't know it then, but soon I would be able to find my way home in the dark.

CHAPTER 14

CRUSADE BRATS

Once they knew what my father did for a living, people liked to boast for us. "Hey, you've gotta meet this family, the Marshalls. Rick Marshall works for Billy Graham!" People always said it that way, going way down in their throats when they said the *G* in Graham, in case people didn't hear them right and thought they said Billy Ham or something. I watched people get excited, get kind of silly, over my dad's job, wishing they had it too.

A lot of times, this happened in Sunday school class. No matter what denomination, the Sunday school teacher (usually in his forties in pressed khakis) would say, "We want to introduce our newest member of class. This is Jessica Marshall. Jessica's dad works for the one and only Billy Graham! What a blessing. Jessica's family has just moved here to get our city ready for Billy Graham's crusades. We are so excited about it. God is going to use your family in mighty ways, young lady."

I couldn't blame people for their enthusiasm. We lived a life touched with a degree of celebrity. I faked humility.

But truth be told, I used my father's position in the BGEA shamelessly to my advantage. My father and his coworkers called me and my siblings "crusade brats"—and for good reason.

Our exploits as crusade brats started the year of the Philadelphia crusade.

Instead of bringing a friend to the crusade that year, I wanted to invite my favorite cousin, Jeff Decker, my Bridgman, Michigan summer sidekick. He wanted to come to Philadelphia and experience a Billy Graham crusade. He'd been told all his life about Uncle Rick's fascinating job.

Every summer, Mom's Decker siblings made Dad tell his BGEA stories over and over again while we all sat around Grammy's big oval dining table.

Jeff had heard these stories. By fourteen, being a smart, sanguine kid he wanted to experience some of that celebrity. Aunt Dar and Uncle Lee agreed and let him fly to Philadelphia that first week in June for crusade week.

I wondered if the cousin Jeff that I saw during our carefree summers in Michigan would be as fun-loving and hilarious in another place. I shouldn't have worried.

From the moment he stepped out of the car and onto our driveway, he had me in stitches. And we caused even more mischief during that week in Philadelphia than we had during any Michigan summer on record.

Jeff, Eric and I pool-hopped around the neighborhood—jumping like slippery frogs—over peoples' fences and into their clean, untouched pools. We stumbled back to our house when the cicadas began tuning up, the light in the sky dimming so fast that we couldn't tell what was tree branch and what was sky. Our eyes bloodshot from chlorine, and our hair like matted straw.

Jeff was a fun companion that first crusade night. He cracked jokes and sang his weird vibrato to the hymns. Part of his charm was that you couldn't tell if he was serious or not. He said and sang everything with gusto and with a politician's charm. I wholly adored him.

At one point during that first night of the crusade, Jeff, Eric, and I thought it would be fun to go explore Veterans Stadium. After all, Jeff said, "Your dad is running this show!"

So we took off from our seats and headed up the tall concrete staircase. But we were abruptly stopped by a small man in thick tortoiseshell glasses. He held out his hand like a traffic cop and said, "Uh, I'm afraid you can't go into this area," at which he pointed a white clammy finger to his lapel badge that read, "Bill Hill: Usher." Eric, Jeff, and I held back our laugher until we returned to our seats, and then we let loose the mockery.

Jeff declared, "I'm going to have a word with Uncle Rick about this *Bill Hill*." Later that night, back at home, Jeff cornered Dad, "Uncle Rick, now, the crusade was interesting and all, and Billy Graham is an incredible speaker, and I was deeply moved by his presentation of the gospel. Don't get me wrong, but I was also very offended tonight. An usher said that we were not allowed to get past him and walk around the stadium." Jeff swept his hand dramatically to indicate Eric and me, the other two victims. I stifled a laugh. Dad grinned too, aware that he was witnessing a performance. But he was also curious enough to keep listening.

"Uncle Rick, you are the director! So I implore you, where are *our* badges? These are the director's children. Why don't they, why don't *we*, have badges? And I don't mean an *usher's* badge," Jeff said, spitting the last two words in disgust. "I mean, *all access*, Uncle Rick. We want the goods, Uncle Rick; we want all access!"

Eric and I leapt from our seats, moved by the politician's demands for reform. "Yeah! We want all access!" Until that moment, I hadn't even known my own needs. Suddenly I could picture it all: the freedom, the importance, the power. Dad chuckled and shook his head, but I could see a glimmer in his blue eyes.

We got our red laminated ALL ACCESS badges from Dad the very next day. "You all are becoming crusade brats," he declared. He may have warned us about such power, but we didn't hear him. There never were brattier, more bothersome, more power-lusty children in all of Billy Graham Evangelistic Association history. Even Billy's own tempestuous, wild grandchildren didn't gloat in their power like we did that week.

On the second night of the crusades, Eric, Jeff, and I, wearing our ALL ACCESS red badges, tore through Veterans Stadium like ransacking soldiers. First we burst into the guest team's locker room, running past some security guards who said we weren't allowed there.

We flashed our badges. They rolled their eyes. But then moved away from the doors to let us through.

We tore into the empty locker room and ran around slamming all the locker doors like overly sugared toddlers. Then it was onto bigger and better things.

Off to the Phillies' locker room. And then after that into the home team's dugout. We needed another high—and fast—so we found some sharp pebbles and dug our initials into the wooden bench in the Phillies' dugout, right where Lenny Dykstra always sat spitting his tobacco juice.

By that time, Billy Graham was up at the pulpit speaking, offering the invitation to well-behaved thousands in the stands. I completely missed my favorite part of the crusade evenings, when the choir sang "Just as I Am." I was busy carving an *M* into the dugout bench.

After Eric, Jeff, and I examined each other's handiwork, Jeff suggested that we ride the elevator to the very tippiest top of Veterans Stadium to get a bird's-eye view. We scampered out of the dugout, flashed our sassy badges to the Bill Hill usher types, found the elevator, and scrambled in. We cackled at our own badness.

There was a man in the elevator already.

He was wearing a navy blue suit and had his hands in his pockets, jingling his loose change the way some men do. He looked a little bit familiar. Maybe I'd met him somewhere. He had a stock smile. He looked humored, but a little weary too.

The man in the elevator looked harmless enough, so I didn't censor myself. "When we get to the top of the stadium, let's spit our gum down into the crowd!" Eric and Jeff smirked, but they glanced warily at the smiling man. I realized that I shouldn't have said that out loud, but it was too late. I was manic in my power.

After the elevator dinged, the man got off at his floor. As he exited, he turned to glance at the three of us one more time.

We did indeed go to the top floor and hurl our Hubba Bubba wads from the top of the stadium and down onto the innocent heads of the gathered Philadelphians. Poor people, wrestling with their eternal fate that night and a wad of gum in their hair.

I didn't give a single other thought to the man in the elevator until late that night, after we came home. Dad turned on the TV to see the local news coverage of the crusade. Sometimes he liked to hear first reports from newscasters— a synopsis of the night's events and the city's reaction—before he crashed into bed.

I was flopped down on the carpet in front of the TV, bone-tired from all the pavement slapping I'd done that night. On the screen, a female newscaster stood outside Veterans Stadium, where we had just been. She was telling the camera that she had Mayor Ed Rendell there to offer us his reaction to the Billy Graham crusade's second night. She turned and the camera panned over slightly to include none other than the man from the elevator.

I shot up off the floor in horror. "That's the mayor?" I yelled.

"Yep, that's him." Dad yawned and turned off the TV. I got up, pale-faced and guilt-stricken.

That night in bed, I confessed all my sins out loud to God before I fell asleep. On the following crusade night, Jeff, Eric, and I tamed down the brat games.

That July, we were, of course, in Bridgman, visiting Grammy and Papa, still not sure where we'd be moving next. One evening, Heather and Dad went for a walk at Weko Beach. Heather started to cry. She told Dad that she wanted to graduate from high school with the same group of friends. She wanted to do at least two years in the same high school. "Can I have that?" she asked him shyly.

Dad's heart broke. He wouldn't lose his children in order to save the world. He didn't say yes to her, but he didn't say no. He didn't say anything. Instead, he hugged his oldest daughter probably like she hadn't let him do in a long time.

A few weeks later, around the kitchen table at Grammy's, Mom and Dad asked us kids if we would like to stay in Philadelphia another year. Would we like to go to the same school again with the same friends, like we did in Rochester? Would we like to stay in the same house for another year? It took a few seconds to register that I was being consulted for my preference on the only matter that mattered in my life. There never was an easier yes.

CHAPTER 15

ONE OF US

We stayed in Newtown Square for another year. The cardboard packing boxes remained in the attic, untouched. As we had done in Rochester, our family stretched into a second year in the same city like carefree cats in the sun. We reveled in a continued sense of place and belonging.

Our home on Wyola Drive was spacious and comfortable, and the neighbors were more entertaining than television. In all our moves around the world, we'd never met more volatile, fascinating people.

Around the corner from us lived Kitty and John Sciotto and their wild brood of eight kids. The Sciottos were the extreme version of everybody in west Philly: hardworking Catholics. And in case you weren't sure they were Italian, their kids' names spelled it out: Johnny, Franco, Kitty-Marie, Louie, Rocco, Salvador, Carmella, and Nicoletta.

John Sciotto was the hardest-working man in town. While fixing the pipes under your kitchen sink, he could tell you a hysterical story about the latest dumb thing one of his hundred kids had done.

His wife, Kitty, was a force to be reckoned with. Everybody feared her. She was a ruthless general in her own house and a coppish bully around town. If she didn't get her coupon discount at the Acme, well, you were gonna hear about it. And if the sorry old man behind her didn't get his discount, well, somebody's manager was gonna hear about it.

She could be a terrifying defender of your rights. She scared people into gratitude. She was the Mafia.

Nobody could curse you out, but nobody could laugh as hard as Kitty Sciotto either. When something struck her funny bone, she laughed so violently that you had better join in too. Kitty never forgot it when somebody made her laugh. If you got Kitty Sciotto to bust a gut, you basically had your own personal Italian bodyguard.

One day in the fall of our second year on Wyola Drive, Eric wandered down to the Sciotto house. With their eight kids, there was always something interesting going on. He stepped around the bikes and footballs that littered the yard. As Eric entered the house, Franco saw him right away and yelled, "Come on, Eric! Johnny's gonna give Rocco a swirly!"

"Louie, Carmella, hold his legs!" Johnny screamed as a helpless Rocco flailed in their arms. The little ones obeyed and gripped Rocco's legs as Johnny directed them all up the stairs. Rocco screamed and cursed, and the others screamed and laughed. Eric had to see this.

Swirlies were something boys often discussed in the locker room, but Eric had never actually witnessed one. In the bathroom upstairs, Johnny had managed to get Rocco turned upside down. Franco and Louie held Rocco's arms behind his back. And just like that, Johnny lowered Rocco's bawling head down into the dingy, yellowed toilet. For one brief moment all was silent. Then Johnny relented and hoisted his brother up and out.

Rocco thrashed, flinging water in every direction like a horse's tail. He cursed with authority and finesse, just like his mother, which is exactly who walked in the front door the very next moment.

The next series of minutes became known to our family as "The Wrath of Kitty Sciotto"—and it turned out that no one was exempt. She tore up the stairs and, in one awe-inspiring swipe, managed to grab hold of every boy's shirt collar in the bathroom, including my brother's. She dragged them like day-old kittens down the stairs and into the open foyer. And before he knew what was happening, Eric Marshall became a Sciotto.

"I'm gone for one hour, buying food for your sorry butts, and this is what I come home to?" She spun and fumed. Rocco's face dripped with dirty water. "I had better have a clean house in one hour, or you'll never step through my front door again."

"Johnny, bathrooms! Franco, garage! Louie, bedrooms! And you, kitchen! Wait, who the heck are you?" Kitty, having gone down the line of brown children, had arrived at my brother. Eric couldn't manage a word. Kitty blinked. Everyone held their breath.

Then Kitty began to laugh. No words came out, just Kitty Sciotto's insane, capricious yowl. She suddenly realized she'd just chewed out the neighbor kid. The stress of eight kids had finally cracked her. She doubled over in laughter, tears welling up in her thick mascara and then streaking black down her cheeks.

Johnny began to snicker too, and then everyone did. Eric managed an injured smile.

"Sorry, man. My mom thought you were one of us." Franco smiled a big apology. Eric let himself out of the house that afternoon, with Kitty Sciotto still howling with laughter in the background.

Eric told us the story over dinner that night, and we all cracked up. Secretly, I treasured the words Franco had said to Eric: "She thought you were one of us." We had never been mistaken for anybody but the new kids, for anybody but the new family in town, for anybody but temporal friends.

Like Mary from the Bible, I stored up the words in my heart. Would we ever really be one of them? the people who made up a community? the constant neighbors down the street? the family, like the Sciottos, whom everybody knew and loved around town?

In the spring of 1993, just after the Pittsburgh crusades (which Dad directed by commuting all week), my parents made the choice that secured our sense of belonging in west Philadelphia.

They bought a house in Newtown Square and announced to their four shocked children that we would never have to move homes again. From that point on, Dad would commute to crusade locations, renting out apartments for five days and then returning to us on weekends. I was sixteen years old; this sacrifice on my parents' part did not register. All I knew was that my dad's announcement was what I had dreamed of hearing all my life.

My parents were both forty-two years old when they bought their first house. Up to that point, they had never painted walls before, had never dug a garden or remodeled a house or hung anything more permanent than a curtain rod.

But all of that changed in just one month. Mom picked out her house on Tyson Road there in Newtown Square. It was a four-bedroom Cape Cod with a finished basement and with the three largest birch trees in the county in the backyard. Mom named our house Three Birches. In a matter of weeks, my family owned a permanent home.

I had seen psychologists over the years for my problem with anxiety. The ones worth their salt summed me up exactly: "The family's transient life has taken its toll on Jess; it seems to be the root of her anxiety."

The root of my anxiety was quite suddenly no longer an issue. The nomadic Marshall family was finally staying put.

My life began to gain traction. You could find me in previous school yearbooks. Boys began to notice my softening profile balancing out into something like prettiness. Teachers recognized my name on their roll, having had my older sister in class. Parents no longer needed to ask where I lived when they gave me a ride home after softball practice.

I got my driver's license the week Mom and Dad bought our house on Tyson Road. Dad bought me a decent, used Honda Accord. I drove my friends all over town. I not only learned the street names in west Philadelphia, I lived them. I became part of what made the place what it was. I was certain that Philadelphia was the home I had been longing for.

The constancy of place worked on me like a tonic, like a million clasps of the hand; it became a hedge, a frame, around my life. My struggles with anxiety virtually vanished.

By our fourth year living in Newtown Square, Philadelphia, that anxiety-ridden girl on the road with the Billy Graham Evangelistic Association seemed a thousand lifetimes away.

Then, in my senior year of high school, I was required by school to write a comprehensive analysis of a poet of my choosing. I chose to write about Bob Dylan and his two albums *Slow Train Coming* and *Saved*, since they had been in part the soundtrack of my childhood.

I began to listen to the albums constantly. During classes, I doodled Bob Dylan's lyrics in the margins of my notebook. I woke up in the morning humming Dylan songs. It was the music I had heard my father play all my life, but only now did I really start to listen.

What I heard Dylan saying in those two albums was crystal clear. After a conversion to Christianity, Bob Dylan had come untethered from a former way of thinking. He'd chosen to wrap his whole mind and heart around a belief in the God of the Bible. In doing so—in unhooking his clasp from the world's ideologies and ambitions—he was losing friends and fans. He was floating away from the world, and he liked it.

> And I walk out on my own
> A thousand miles from home
> But I don't feel alone
> 'Cause I believe in you.

It was all right there. Because of Bob Dylan's faith in Christ, the world no longer held his heart. I comprehended this, and it unsettled me.

As I began to craft my essay, I realized that the very music that had soothed my fearful heart as we traveled between cities with Billy Graham was now challenging me.

Dylan was proclaiming with relief, *This world is not my home.* Personally, I couldn't ignore the message.

Just when I finally had license to claim a geographic home on the map, just when I finally put down roots, his music whispered to my soul the truth of Scripture: *Love this place loosely. Heaven is your real home.*

I had thought I wanted to be "one of us," to belong in every way to a community of people with a latitude and longitude on terra firma.

But Jesus said, "I go to prepare a place for you. If it wasn't true, I wouldn't say it."

That meant, with Christ as my savior, the home I longed for was still to come. I could live in Newtown Square, Pennsylvania my whole life, but it still wouldn't be the home He meant for me.

CHAPTER 16

THE VISIONARY AND THE POET: MY FATHER'S FINAL CRUSADE

I grew up knowing that my father was a gifted man. I had seen him direct Billy Graham crusades, had heard him preach to rapt crowds, and had watched him give his powerful testimony of salvation in Christ. I never tired of his story.

I loved it because it was raw and true. Dad liked musicians for the same reasons. Some of them—like Bob Dylan and John Lennon—were poets. And poets, my father taught me, were close to the heart of God.

During a particularly surly stage of high school, I blurted out to my father, "There's nothing interesting for my friends at a Billy Graham crusade." Immediately I wished I hadn't said it. Dad's face fell. I had hurt him, and I wished badly to take it back, but it was the truth. I was embarrassed to bring my friends to a Billy Graham crusade. My teenage ego cringed at the outdated hymns, at the pacing of the event and the conservative rhetoric.

My father didn't forget my stinging rebuke of his work. In fact, my comment became the impetus for massive changes he implemented during his last years with the BGEA.

In early 1993, Dad began to research the demographics of church and crusade attendance. What he found was not encouraging. Crusade attendance had been in steady decline in North America.

The generation born in the late seventies and early eighties were largely outside the Church's grasp. The seeker-friendly megachurches were mostly disinterested in BGEA crusade evangelism. They respected Billy but had no interest in applying the now outdated methods attributed to Billy's past successes in reaching audiences with the gospel.

Dad found himself at a crossroads. He couldn't ignore his realizations, but he was deeply committed to helping Billy Graham finish his years of evangelism well, and that meant staying employed by the BGEA a little while longer.

Just after the Pittsburgh crusade, in the fall of 1993, Rob Catchcant, executive director of Youth for Christ, said to Dad, "You guys in the BGEA are dinosaurs—you aren't really doing anything to reach the youth." It was a statement that made Dad mad, mad enough that he couldn't ignore his ideas any longer. It brought to mind my earlier criticisms. He turned to Cliff Barrows first, just hoping for an open mind.

"Cliff, what if we amped things up, added some high-energy music to the crusades?" He went on to describe his ideas for music and advertising that might appeal to younger audiences.

Cliff back-stepped. "I can't authorize that, Rick! You have to talk to Billy."

So Dad went to the man himself. From a pay phone, Dad finally caught Billy. The phone reception was terrible, but Dad knew that moments of Billy's undivided attention were rare. He wouldn't have another chance to share his heart, so he barreled through the static "Mr. Graham, I want to tell you something that's been on my mind!" He took a deep breath and prayed for courage. "We aren't reaching teenagers. They don't come to our crusades. We need to make the crusades something your grandchildren would want to attend. I'm talking about music, loud music. I'm talking about concerts. And then, of course, the straight, honest gospel message from you to them." There was a long static pause. Dad held his breath.

"Why, music! That's nothing, Rick! Back when Ruth and I worked for Youth for Christ, we rented a hundred grand pianos and put them on the stage at Chicago's McCormick Place. And talking horses, Rick! Ask the horse a Bible question, and it would paw once for 'yes' and twice for 'no.'"

Dad cringed. Clydesdales and Howdy Doody weren't quite what he had in mind. Mr. Graham kept going. "We'd call out seat numbers for kids to come down to the stage and sit on toilet seats ..." Dad began to feel sick with discouragement.

But then he realized what Billy wasn't saying but was trying to convey: that he would do whatever it took to share the gospel with the next generation. The man had a long history of taking risks to share the gospel. In essence, radical methods were nothing new to him. He was willing to take a risk.

"Mr. Graham, we don't need talking horses or toilet seats this time, but we will have the stuff that interests teenagers right now—loud music and a message."

There was another long, static pause, but this time Dad wasn't worried.

"Let's do it, Rick."

Dad thanked Mr. Graham and then dialed his longtime secretary, Suzanne Byrne. "Suzanne, put it in writing with today's date: Billy said yes."

It was the fall of 1993. In Billy's forty-five years of ministry, his team had never arranged an evangelical event targeted for an audience of a specific age group. There was much debate about that. Isn't the gospel message enough to draw any demographic? But my father, unlike many BGEA board members, had teenagers. And one of them had said that there was nothing to make people of her age bracket *want* to attend a Billy Graham event.

Dad knew the ins and outs of directing the classic version of Billy Graham crusades, but flipping one to reflect a rock concert was entirely new to him. He grappled and improvised and faked his way to mission week. The rock and hip-hop stations in Cleveland advertised the event for months, "Introducing the first concert to benefit its own audience, featuring DC Talk and Michael W. Smith, and a message from Reverend Billy Graham." It all sounded official, but Dad honestly had no idea what to expect.

Michael W. Smith, darling of Christian contemporary music in the 1980s, beloved by housewives and benign youth pastors across the United States, was an easy choice for the second act of the Youth Night concerts. The first band would be DC Talk, formed early in the nineties. They were just edgy enough to interest non-Christian teenagers, and yet their lyrics clearly pointed to a personal relationship with Christ, which was essential to Billy's message. Their first album, *Free at Last*, featured a song that got played on the non-Christian radio station, which was important for advertising.

The Cleveland crusades would be held at Cleveland's Municipal Stadium, and the first ever BGEA Youth Night would be on Saturday evening, June 11.

When the slated night arrived, thirty thousand people waited outside the stadium doors for three hours to get in. It was exciting and disastrous all at once. Dad surveyed the writhing mass of teenagers on the faux green turf and knew that the group was beyond his control. All he could do was add more ushers at the front. Kids pressed the rope in anticipation of their new favorite Christian rock band. The final attendance count that night was sixty-five thousand.

That was the scene I first glimpsed when I stepped through the tunnel at tier 2 and walked into the stadium. I blinked, not sure what I was actually seeing. For a second it seemed that I was at the wrong event. This was a concert. The geriatric version of the Billy Graham crusades I'd grown up attending had to be going on somewhere else. This was mayhem barely in check.

I turned to Mom and said, "Whoa, this is different."

Mom only grinned and laughed. "Yep!"

And then we began our perfunctory scanning of the crowds for Dad. I wanted to have a word with my Dad about all this. Was Billy Graham really going to speak tonight? I couldn't conceive of it. Hip-hop blasted from the jumbo speakers and little tornado mosh pits erupted like dust devils on the stadium floor.

As it turned out, Dad was busy sidestepping catastrophes. He had placed Mr. Graham in a quiet room deep in the interior of the stadium. Sometimes Mr. Graham would meet and pray with certain dignitaries or friends in makeshift greenrooms before going out to speak. He liked to have a television in the room so that he could watch and listen to the choir sing some pleasant worship music to encourage him.

But Dad had had a premonition about that first Youth Night: it was going to be loud. Just moments before Mr. Graham was ushered into his little greenroom, Dad stole in and ripped out the audio cords from the TV set.

About a half hour into DC Talk's performance, Dad peaked into the small room and saw Billy's assistant T. W. Wilson pounding on the TV set. "Somebody get in here! I can't get any sound out of this thing! Is that man climbing the speaker tower? What in the world is going on out there?"

Dad slipped away as quietly as possible.

Indeed, Toby McKeehan, lead singer and band leader of DC Talk, had climbed up the left sound tower, fifty feet above the stadium floor. The audience loved it. Kids and freewheeling adults screamed and aahed at his bravado. I sat with my jaw slack, completely shocked by what I was witnessing at a Billy Graham crusade. *Now this was something I could bring my friends to see.*

It was often Dad's job to escort Mr. Graham out to the stage. Depending on how well Billy could walk that night, Dad sometimes used a golf cart to get him there. It was one of those nights.

Dad drove Mr. Graham out the last tunnel that led to the stage, and Billy caught a glimpse of the crowds. "Rick! What's that they're doing?" Mr. Graham asked, alarmed.

Dad looked up warily at the crowd doing the wave around the entire stadium. "Uh, that's a new wave of prayer, sir."

DC Talk ended their last song drenched in sweat. They turned toward the right side of the stage as Mr. Graham was helped up the steps by security. Toby reached out, grabbed hold of Mr. Graham's hand, and helped him the rest of the way toward center stage. The other two band members came forward. All three of them reached out to embrace Mr. Graham in the kind of hug you give your grandfather. Toby's head bent to touch Billy's shoulder for the briefest of seconds. And Mr. Graham hugged them back.

Sixty-five thousand people looked on and cheered. Then DC Talk stepped away and went back to the seating area reserved for musical guests.

I held my breath, surveying my peers in the thousands there that night. How would they react to the man who had shaped the trajectory of my life? How would they respond to his message about Christ? How would they feel about this man who was growing so much older every time I watched him speak, whose hair whitened more every year and was now the color of a dove's wing, who had pressed his thick, dry hand on my head and had prayed for my life when I was eleven?

Then he held up that same hand as if to direct a rowdy puppy. "That's enough now," he said, a smile on his weathered face. And just like that, the masses sat down. Kids my age who were, a second before, throwing themselves at the stage barricades now sat down in stilled attention.

Then Billy Graham walked gingerly to the podium with that signature black Bible of his and leaned over to speak into the microphone.

The harvest is ripe, but the workers are few and afraid. Dad called Billy Graham the youngest old man he'd ever met, the only one within the craggy machine of the BGEA's organization whose heart burned to reach all people with a simple story of freedom. Mr. Graham was the only one willing to risk his reputation in the face of the big donors. He was the one with the most to lose, the one whose reputation actually might have mattered, the only one whose name was on the thing.

All the other men in the BGEA cowered in fear at the volume of music. They remained mealymouthed in interviews, noncommittal. They were silly men who talked around board room tables about being too worldly, people who wouldn't and couldn't recognize a thing of beauty, a new thing, an artistic expression, if it smacked them in the face or if looked like a grungy teenager.

In March of 1995, Dad was in Puerto Rico for another BGEA mission that would be broadcast around the world. Billy and Ruth were there staying at a beachside villa. Billy called Dad at his hotel room. "Rick, I want you to come to my villa this evening. Ruth and I want to talk to you."

The lush black trees brushed the taxi windows as it coiled through the winding beachfront streets. Dad stepped into the rickety villa and found Billy out back on the veranda with his Bible open to Psalm 71. Ruth was in the kitchen.

"I'll make some tea," she said.

Dad sat down next to Billy at the patio table.

"There's a lot of controversy, Rick, over what you are doing in the organization," Billy stated in his simple, blunt way.

"But don't be sorry!" Ruth called out from the kitchen.

Billy sat loosely, relaxed. "Rick, I'm going to read you something." And he began to read from Psalm 71:

> Since my youth, O God, you have taught me,
> and to this day I declare your marvelous deeds.
> Even when I am old and gray,
> do not forsake me, O God,
> till I declare your power to the next generation,
> your might to all who are to come.

"Tell him about the fuddy-duddies!" Ruth called out from the kitchen. Billy, tell him how we swore that we wouldn't become like them."

Billy smiled. "Well, she's right." Dad was humbled and grateful. It was Billy's way of affirming the Youth Nights that Dad had set in motion.

Though his family lived in Newtown Square, Pennsylvania, my father still traveled with Billy Graham. He still organized local churches and taught evangelism classes in each city that held a Billy Graham crusade event. He still worked with local leaders and advertising firms to promote the BGEA events. But the Youth Nights, having been his visionary concept, became the compelling focus of all his preparations in the last years of the millennium.

From that first Youth Night event in Cleveland, in June 1994, the BGEA went on to conduct twenty-two similar events, ending in Oklahoma City in June 2003. In total, 1,286,500 people attended the Youth Night events and heard the gospel spoken by Mr. Graham. Of the twenty-two events, twelve broke the all-time stadium records for attendance.

As a teenager, I attended the Youth Nights that my father orchestrated, and my childhood affection for him turned to admiration. I began to love him in a new way because he wanted his teenage children and their friends to hear the gospel of good news in mediums they would respect. In my dad's last twelve years with Billy Graham, he worked tirelessly to that effect with much criticism.

Dad was never afraid of art, of those who pursued it. He was never afraid of the radical, and certainly not of change. For over eleven years, he had packed up his family every nine months and moved us like alley pups, all because one man asked him to. Dad was dichotomous, questioning authority and yet staking our future on the authority of one man's calling to preach the gospel around the world. And we were to help him.

By 2001, Billy was in poor spirits almost continuously. He confessed to Dad that he was daunted by the new generation, the technology onslaught, and the pace of the media. It all buffeted him like a relentless wave. He doubted that anyone under thirty would want to hear him speak. He labored under the fear that he had nothing new to tell them.

He often said that he only knew one story, and he wasn't sure he could communicate even that anymore. As a result, Dad's role in the BGEA took on a gentler tone; he became a kind of rallying friend to Billy, doing his best to encourage him. They wrote letters to one another.

Over and over again, Dad reminded Billy in letters that young and old people needed to hear him preach. Furthermore, many people wanted to meet with him for encouragement because he was a man of integrity. As it turned out, one of those people was Bono of U2.

It was the right sort of collision, the kind where someone with a gift collides with someone with a need. It was the collision that my father was not able to orchestrate twenty years earlier with a different poet, Bob Dylan. This time, the details fell into place with perfect grace.

In early 2001, as Billy reeled under discouragement, Dad expressed an idea to Billy's assistant David Bruce. For years, Dad had envisioned a meeting between Billy Graham and Bono. Bono was at the center of every world peacekeeping work. U2's music through the years continued a narrative of personal spirituality, often times directly stating a belief in Christ. Bono was a man of heart and compassion, and he was a poet.

Anybody who watched the news could see it, not to mention hear it in every song. He was a man of depth. It seemed natural that Bono and Billy Graham should meet.

David Bruce mentioned that Dad should tell his idea to Tedd Smith, BGEA's longtime musical director. So Dad did, and it turned out that Tedd was close friends with Steve Turner, English music journalist, poet, and longtime friend of Bono. With Ted's help, Dad got ahold of Steve, who confirmed what Dad had sensed in his heart for many years: that as a believer in Christ, Bono was eager to spend personal time with Billy Graham.

For once, it was a stadium event that Dad had no part in organizing. It was a stop in Lexington, Kentucky, on U2's *All that You Can't Leave Behind* tour in 2001. As arranged by e-mail, Dad would meet Bono and the rest of the band prior to their concert to coordinate a time to meet with Billy Graham.

Around 6:00 p.m., Dad waited at the lip of an interior tunnel, like every sports stadium in America, a gray tunnel leading to the band's greenroom. As he stood waiting, Dad thought about how many times he'd ushered in waiting guests who were standing awkwardly like he was now in this same spot, ready to meet Billy. Now he was that guest.

Bono emerged from a doorway dressed in mostly black, his trademark sunglasses propped on his head. He was straight-faced and had a purposeful walk. Dad reached out to shake his hand, but Bono embraced him instead. "Brother, you have been sent by the Lord."

It shocked Dad, but he regained himself and did his best to fill in some details for the man about Billy's current health and emotional condition.

"Hold on a minute." Bono interrupted and took Dad's arm, leading him toward U2's greenroom.

Inside were some of the others, the Edge, Larry Mullen, and Jack Heaslip, the last a pastor from the band members' old school days in Dublin. "Edge, come here. I want you to meet this guy." The Edge, quiet, wearing a soft expression, and clad in black ski hat, came and stood quietly next to Bono.

Bono began. "We don't understand the American church, and we don't think she understands us. We are not an evangelical band; we are a prophetic band." And then he added, "The thing I long for most in my life is a blessing. If what you say is true, Rick, I will go anywhere at any time to meet with Billy Graham."

And then Bono prayed for my father.

On March 11, 2002, at Billy's beloved home in the Black Mountains of North Carolina, Billy Graham and Bono sat and talked like old friends on Billy's front porch. A month later, Dad received a letter in the mail from Steve Turner. Steve had written the following:

> I had a letter from Bono a couple of weeks back telling me about the meeting with Billy and Ruth. He said that he had received the blessing from it that he had wanted, so I am pleased that eventually everything went as you had wanted and the whole thing was worth while. I have noticed a deepening of spiritual maturity in the little glimpses I get, which I think is a good sign because the terrible tendency of people in the public eye like this is to grow "cold" as time passes. Bono is a real encouragement that although there is one Lord, one baptism and one Spirit there are many ways to be an obedient believer. I'm glad he didn't get put into a straight jacket too early.

I grew up thinking that my father was famous because his favorite music was famous and so was his boss. And somewhere in the middle was my life and my longing for a sense of home.

In 2004 the elements of my conceptions came to an abrupt end when my dad resigned from his work with the Billy Graham Evangelistic Association.

When people asked me why, all I could say was, "My dad felt called to work for Billy, not for his son." It was the short answer, and it was the best angle I could understand.

By 2005 Billy Graham had already preached the gospel of hope in Jesus Christ to millions all over the globe. He was called "America's pastor." He had known every president since Eisenhower intimately. But he needed help for one last crusade. In May 2005, one month before the New York City crusade, Billy wrote the following to my dad:

> Rick, as I prepare for New York if you have any
> illustrations or stories I could use, I would really
> appreciate it. I need you to help me with your vision
> and application of truth. I don't have many that I
> can turn to for help like I can to you. You are still
> very important to my life and ministry.

With that request, Dad put together a packet of material with a variety of illustrations gleaned to communicate effectively to a New York City audience. The day before the last crusade meeting was held in Madison Square Garden, Dad received a note from Billy's secretary, Stephanie Wills. It read as follows: "Thanks for holding up the boss's arms—he really seemed encouraged to have your material to read through over and over. One more to go—and perhaps this is the 'finishing well' sermon!"

CHAPTER 17

A STORY ABOUT YOU

Imagine yourself as one of thousands and thousands of people streaming in through the doors of a giant arena. You spent yourself arriving—the traffic, the parking, the throng of strangers. The people here don't look like you, but you keep moving forward. High up near the gathering stars are empty seats; no one goes there, it is too dark, too remote. You climb away from the others and move toward those distant seats. It seems years to get there. The stadium lights are bright and searching; it takes all your effort to keep moving.

You don't want to be here, but it's too hard to leave now.

Finally you find that seat farthest from the crowd; the arena below whirls in movement. Some people are still streaming in; others, drifting around the green turf floor. You wait; it seems you wait forever.

After all the singing and clapping, the prayers by esteemed leaders, then the man you've heard about enters from the back of the stage.

He isn't what you expected; he doesn't hold his head up and wave broadly like a politician. He watches his brown shoes as he approaches the podium, his footing unsteady. You wonder why you came. This man can't help you. He can hardly walk.

Then he lifts a shaking right arm to signal for quiet. In such a cavernous place, it is the merest gesture, but everyone stops their noise. No one speaks. No one claps. Then he begins, "I would like to read you a story." He opens the Bible and reads. It's a very old story.

The voice doesn't match the look of the man. His voice is not fragile. His voice is like a man's in a wooden boat on still water at sunset. By some miracle you hear every word from miles away. Soon you have forgotten yourself enough to consider the message. He does not plead or threaten with fear, but he asks you to listen.

And then he stops speaking.

Now it is as if the stadium empties and it is he and you and maybe four or five others who also sit high and alone or buried in the crowd of thousands. He gathers the six of you around him the way a fisherman and his crew sit close together around the fire on a shore. He tells you to listen to the story again. He says that the story is about you.

He looks down and waits, because it is no small thing to have a story be yours. Your eyes burn with recognition.

What happens next is a mystery.

You might remember how your steps going down matched the rhythm in your chest. It might be that your eyes filled. You might have had your arms crossed or to your sides. You might have said "Excuse me" to someone blocking the path. You make your way down, closer and closer to the front.

The man at the podium waits for you. He measures your pace and waits. When you are finally there in front, he says, "Friend, I am so glad you have come." He tells you to bow your head. You do and say to God that you are sorry in a way that makes you cry and for things very bitter in your life.

You ask Jesus to come and be with you, because He promised that He would. You ask Him to build His home inside you. You cough and cry; someone next to you touches your back softly. You cry for a long time, and the hand stays there on your back.

It seems a very long time passes. Much of what used to be doesn't seem to matter anymore. You tilt your head back and open your new eyes. The man is not at the podium anymore. He is seated on a stool with his head bent down, his hands covering his face. He prays.

You breathe one more time in that place, a long, newly awakened breath. Then you step out into the advancing dawn.

Blackbird singing in the dead of night.
Take these broken wings and learn to fly.
All your life,
You were only waiting for this moment
To arise.

—The Beatles

CHAPTER 18

MY LAST CRUSADE

The summer after I graduated from Millersville University with a degree in English, I attended my last Billy Graham crusade. It was Cincinnati, Ohio, in 2002, and I didn't know it would be my final glimpse of the man whose calling to preach the gospel had shaped my childhood. On the final night of the crusade week, I sat in a private box seat, high up above the stadium crowd.

I was gathered with my immediate family and with several cousins and aunts and uncles from the Kentucky area. That night, my cousins had brought some friends of theirs to the crusade—a family with two young children, a boy and a girl. The family lived deep in the woods of rural Kentucky and told me how little they had experienced in life. The little girl said on our ride up the escalator to the box seats that she "had never been on one of these before," pointing down at the escalator.

The view of the stadium from the box seats was perfect. I relaxed into a very familiar service, listening tenderly to the icons of my youth: Tedd Smith on piano, Cliff Barrows, and good ol' George Beverly Shea. I knew that soon Billy Graham would be escorted out by Dad to speak.

In one month I would be moving again, this time by my own volition, to teach English in Taiwan. I didn't know it that night, but in one week I would meet for the first time the man who would become my husband. The open air stadium let in great, sweeping gusts of fresh summer breezes. As I listened and watched, a sense of immanent beauty made me shiver with expectation.

After the musical portion of the service, there was some murmuring around me. My mom leaned over to me and whispered, "Jess, this little boy wants to meet Third Day." It was the little boy from the rural Kentucky family. "Why don't you take him down to meet his favorite band?"

I looked at Mom and blinked. It had been years since I'd roamed around a stadium flashing an ALL ACCESS badge, and I told her as much. Mom didn't reply. She just tilted her head in a way that always meant, *I think you'll figure it out.*

I sat for a minute and considered, and then I got up out of my seat and took the little boy's hand in mine. In his other hand he held his camera.

I walked him out of the room, took him down the concrete hall, and then walked over to the escalator. We rode it in silence down to the ground floor, the stadium floor. We came to a tunnel leading out onto the field, and my heart skipped a beat. The lights up ahead were forceful and intimidating; for a moment I hesitated. But I held the boy's hand and decided to walk with purpose like my father had always taught me. He'd taught me to walk confidently through every airport, through the halls of a hundred new schools, and down the length of a hundred new streets where we had lived.

And suddenly, as I walked, I realized what had given my parents intrepid hearts to live the life we had lived for fifteen years.

Once I had made the decision, walking forward was easy. I walked steadily, the boy holding my hand for direction. I walked out onto the false turf of the stadium floor, out into the piercing lights, toward a new and ancient story unfolding for me and for thousands of souls there that night.

I knew the way, and no one stopped me. I needed no badge anymore. We walked straight through security barricades and then rounded the corner of the stage. I saw Billy Graham waiting in the wings to be escorted to the podium, and at the sight of him my heart swelled like the plumage of a bird before it ascends. He would tell the people how to get home.

Like me, it might take them years to understand, but if they believed, they would come to know that home is both the One who calls us and the place He is preparing. One day, He will be waiting for me as I run the length of a glowing street to meet Him. He will be up ahead, and the house behind Him will be mine forever.

The boy and I walked right up to the musicians in the band, sitting and talking backstage. I asked them if the boy could have his picture taken with them. They welcomed him, and I took the photograph. No one stopped me.

I must have looked just like my father.

Jess Archer is a freelance writer. She lives in Austin, Texas, with her singer-songwriter husband, B. Sterling Archer, and their two children. Archer is a member of the Writer's League of Texas.

Printed in the United States
By Bookmasters